Mother Mary's Resurrection

A Businessman's Awakening Through Our Universal Mother

Alex Gutierrez

Puzzleworks L.L.C
P.O. Box 300
Sedona, AZ 86339-0300

LCCN 2009922711
ISBN-10 0-9823243-0-8
ISBN-13 978-0-9823243-0-1

Cover Design: Graphics by Manjari and Andres Gutierrez
Cover Painting: Raisa Goltsin
Manuscript Editing: Beatriz Closa
Copy Editing: Sue Ducharme
Interior Design: J. L. Saloff
Typography: Garamond Premier Pro, Palatino, Cochin

Grateful acknowledgment is made to Centro Editoriale Valtortiano s.r.l., Isola del Liri (FR), Italy, the publisher of the following books: *The Poem of the Man God by Maria Valtorta; The Book of Azariah by Maria Valtorta*; and *The Virgin Mary in the Writings of Maria Valtorta* by Fr. Gabriel Roschini, O.S.M.; and for granting permission to quote copy-righted material, to whom all rights for Maria Valtorta's complete works are reserved. All bible quotes are from the King James Version, unless otherwise noted.

v. 1.02
First Edition, 2009
Printed on acid free paper.

Contents

I dedicate this book to my mother and father,
who taught me the best rule of all:
Never do unto others what you don't want done unto you,
and provided for me a "perfectly functional family."
To all my children who have supported me
all the way through this project
and, in one way or another, helped bring it to completion.
And to my family and friends, especially those who have
been there for me in those difficult moments.

Acknowledgments

This book would not have been possible without the help of my wife Beatriz. Not only has she stood by my side during this project (my first book), watching our limited bank savings dwindle, but she has added her amazing wisdom to each page of the book. Beatriz was my sounding board and helped me capture the ideas; she was my editor, making my tedious writing more interesting for you; and she was instrumental in making Mary such an important part in my life.

My deepest gratitude and eternal love to you, Beatriz.

Introduction

The book you are about to read is written from the perspective of a simple and curious man trying to figure out the meaning of life. I do not pretend to be an expert Marian scholar, nor an experienced writer. In fact, this is my first book. But I believe my merit lies in making this book simple and relevant, with universal appeal.

Until recently, I was a top executive of a successful and growing international business, but for reasons you will soon discover, I voluntarily stepped down to write this book about Mother Mary. After many years of self-discovery, prompted among other things by the possibility of my death, I traveled a dual path of meditation and faith, to first heal my emotional body and then my physical body. Along this path I discovered Mary.

Mary's story is extraordinary, but most of us have not been exposed to many aspects of Her life. If we only knew, it would have a radical impact on our opinion of Her. Mary is appearing in many places in the world, but few people are really paying attention to Her messages. Mary has appeared more in the last few decades than in all the previous nineteen centuries. Why? Just coincidences? Does this have any relation with the approaching year 2012, which the Mayas anticipated to be the end of an important cosmic cycle for the Earth? We will discuss these important questions later in the book; but the fact that this phenomenon of the apparitions is taking place and people are not paying attention confirms most people don't really know Mary.

The picture I will paint of Mary reflects what I can now see in this jigsaw puzzle that I have been building for over ten years. This jigsaw puzzle had no box cover, and therefore when I started I did not know what the image would look like. Some parts are now recognizable, but I continue searching for the missing pieces every day.

I want Mary to be known to the common people. I want Mary to be part of the everyday life of young people, business people, housewives bringing up children—not just a part of devout elder ladies' devotions. Mary is much more than just another porcelain vase decoration.

Mary shook the very essence of my being. The more I knew Her, the more I wanted to know about Her. The more I discovered Her, the more I fell in love with Her. The search for Mary has allowed me to truly discover the essence of my faith. Without Mary, I would have never been able to get to where I am today. Don't get me wrong; Jesus has done and continues to do wondrous things in my life, but it was through exploring Mary that I learned more and began to better understand my purpose on Earth.

You see, I am an engineer, and for me it is difficult to just accept things without understanding the rationale behind them. I am sure this feeling will resonate with lots of people. But Mary helped me find the rationale behind my faith, and this in turn increased my faith tenfold. I believe my findings can be useful to other people as well, and this is why I was compelled to make a bold change in the course of my life and write this book—a simple and easy to read book that would bring Mary, this incredible person, back to life.

This book gathers the relevant information about Mary's life from many different sources, including: scripture, oral tradition captured in dogmas, and private revelation that fills in gaps that have prevented us from knowing Her well. If the information from private revelation—another term for visions and channeled information—was relevant and came from a reputable source, and it matched oral tradition, it made it to the book.

Many times I placed myself in meditation and asked for clarity about particular issues. The response would come to my mind and help me sort through the various theories and positions. This personal experience is to me an important value, because once your heart is filled with Mary, She will find ways to get through to you the messages you require at the time. This is true for me and anyone with experience in meditation. Most importantly, because I am not a theologian or a scholar or a Church authority, I can write about things that such people would be unable to write. I have no affiliation with any institution and do not have to respond to anyone but God and myself for my writings.

Some information in this book may be very obvious to the educated scholar, but I believe it will be useful to the ordinary person without formal religious education. And even if you have had a formal religious education, if it is anything like I have seen over the last ten years, then probably you will find in this book interesting and relevant information that you wished you had known a long time ago.

Throughout most of the book I incorporate quotes and references from two extraordinary visionaries: Anne Catherine Emmerich and Maria Valtorta. The writings of both of these women have received positive comments from Church authorities, who have said that nothing in them contradicts sacred scripture and therefore can be used to enrich our faith. I always find it amazing some people are willing to believe and follow ideas which are quite questionable without any hesitation and then reject ideas that come from highly spiritual, reputable human beings on the basis on some superficial rational analysis. Some people, for example, still question the holiness of Anne Catherine Emmerich, who was able to live for twelve years without any food, just by nourishing her body with the Holy Eucharist and water. Let me repeat, in case you missed it. Twelve years without any food!

We will discuss the meaning of some of Mary's recent messages and how they have played a role in my life. Although messages come from Mary in many different places in the world where she currently appears or has recently appeared, I chose the messages coming from Medjugorje, in Eastern Europe, as the most representative. Medjugorje is the most important site of Marian apparitions right now and seems the best choice. Mary's messages from other places are similar and consistent with those in Medjugorje.

I ask the reader to meditate on the messages of Mary presented here. They are very simple, but with deep content. Because of their simplicity, it is easy to pass them by without noticing or realizing their significance. So find some quiet time and meditate on what these messages mean to you as you are reading the book. Now, let us begin our journey and our discovery of Mary.

Chapter 1

Losing Enlightenment

My journey to self-discovery began in 1997, in a most profound way. I had to reach the bottom of the barrel of my life to start remaking it anew. For several years before that, I was just another arrogant, high-level corporate executive, working for a multinational company, climbing the corporate ladder of power and ego, feeling on top of the world.

But in my insatiable desire for success, this was not enough. I wanted to translate my success in the corporate world to success in the entrepreneurial world. So I left this job and all its future potential to start a company on my own. I thought of myself so highly at that time that there was no doubt in my mind that I was going to be extremely successful and the envy of many.

Reality proved to be different, and it slapped me right in my face. The new business was not going as well as anticipated, and I could not fully support my family financially. I then started having problems in my marriage, which by then had produced three beautiful children. This ended up in separation and eventually a divorce. But the worst was yet to come.

Early in April 1997 came the day I discovered I had cancer. What was happening to my life? My work, my marriage, and my health were all crumbling! For me, it is now a fact that many physical illnesses start in our emotional bodies before reaching our physical bodies. The emotional effects of my separation took their toll in my body.

I had been to the doctor for a small discomfort I was feeling. I never imagined it could be cancer. After an ultrasound test, the doctor explained to me in a serious tone that I had a cancerous tumor, of the worst type, and that I needed to have it removed immediately. He recommended I stay in the hospital that night and have the procedure performed the next morning. It was that urgent. Silence on my part followed. I was in complete shock.

That night, when I was alone in my room, pondering the events, a wonderful smiling lady in her late fifties entered my room and asked me if I wanted to take communion. I believed in God then and was taught good values by my parents, but I was not an active Christian. Growing up, my family did not go to church, except for weddings and baptisms. So I knew very little about my faith, and much less about the sacraments.

When this lady asked me if I wanted to take communion, my face must have gone completely white. In my ignorance, I thought that she was giving me the communion that they give to people who are about to die. I thought to myself, "It must be worse than I thought. I may not come out of this one alive." I accepted the host, for in the lonely and miserable state I was in, God was reaching out for me.

In the cold hospital room, I asked God for forgiveness and cried my soul out. How was it possible that I had allowed my life to get to this miserable state? I had always thought of myself as someone special, someone who had been blessed with a lot of talents and who was going to make a difference in the world. But there I was, lying in that hospital bed, contemplating the possible end of my life.

The operation the following morning was a success. The tumor was completely removed. But my life would never be the same again. The doctor then recommended chemotherapy and/or radiotherapy to make sure that my body was clean of any cancerous cells. I instead opted for another approach. Those treatments did not resonate well in my mind; I felt that there had to be a better way to heal oneself than bombarding your body with toxic substances. My father had died of cancer several years earlier, and I had investigated alternative healing methods back then.

One of the cancer treatments that gained my attention was provided by Dr. Atkins in his New York clinic. Yes, this was the same doctor who shortly would become famous with the Atkins diet for weight loss. So I went to New York and submitted myself to all sorts of tests. They even tested my hair for heavy metals.

After all the results were in, I met with Dr. Atkins, and he gave me his treatment, consisting of several herb extracts, minerals, vitamins, and the complete elimination of carbohydrates, sugar, alcohol, and caffeine from my diet. I followed this strict diet, drank the infusions, and swallowed the pills for over a year, and I felt it was working for me, although I was losing a lot of weight.

My new journey had begun. Living alone brought a new dimension to my life. I started reading and meditating. I searched the self-help section of the book stores and discovered authors who would have a great impact in my recovery, like Deepak Chopra, with his Quantum Healing. I meditated every day for an hour and felt I was defeating cancer.

In my meditations, I would visualize a cleansing process that pushed all cancerous cells down to my feet and out of my body. At the same time, the sole of my feet were scaling, and black dots, like old splinters, came out. This clearly reaffirmed the effectiveness of my treatment. The CAT scans and blood tests every four months were coming back with good results. Dr. Atkins' treatment and my meditations were working! During this time I learned a lot about how to heal the body. But something was still missing.

Then, in late 1997, I was invited to attend a Catholic Retreat in Miami. I wasn't too keen on going, but when I learned that this retreat was conducted by men just like me, without the participation of priests, I decided to go. I felt a strong rejection at the time to the concept of a retreat conducted by priests. What could they know about life challenges, beyond what they hear in confessions? I can confidently say that it was in this retreat that I really met Christ for the first time; the being I would come to love so much.

While I was discovering Christ, I also continued with my meditations, which were working so effectively. I found a way to combine my new prayers to Christ with my meditations. I started reading about the history of philosophy and read the summarized life stories of Kant, Descartes, and several other philosophers.

I was so hungry for understanding the meaning of life and my newfound faith that I would read anything that could lead me to discover a missing piece of my puzzle. I read Karen Armstrong's *History of God*, which gave me perspective into other religions, including Islam and Jewish religions. I read Thomas Cahill's *The Gift of the Jews*, which shed light on the history of Jewish patriarchs. I read about physics and the formation of the universe by authors such as Michael Talbot, Alan Wolf, and Stephen Hawking.

I then started serving in Emmaus retreats and met Landy Silva, a Miami oncologist, who through his behavior and life examples introduced me to Mother Mary. Landy had a true devotion to Mary, and he referred to Her with much love and tenderness. There was a clear difference in his devotion compared to what I had seen in other people. I suddenly wanted to experience that feeling for myself, so I started by praying the Rosary every day.

I also began reading the saints. I found out how these people had endured difficulties in their lives and had discovered God. I read Saint Augustine, Saint Francis of Assisi, Saint Catherine of Siena, Saint Bridget, Saint Theresa of Avila, Blessed Anne Catherine Emmerich, and a few others. Each one of the books I read gave me a piece of my jigsaw puzzle and offered information that was satiating my thirst.

In 2001, right after the 9/11 attacks on the World Trade Center, I met Beatriz, who would later become my wife. Beatriz is also devoted to Mary and embodies so many of the qualities of Mary: unconditional love, wisdom, and purity of heart. Her life has been surrounded by events related to Mary, and this made me ever more curious about the Mother and revealed another spiritual dimension that I had missed.

Beatriz has been close to Mary since she was a little girl. The scent of flowers would appear around her frequently, and still does occasionally, and this means the real presence of Mary is close to her. I have myself smelled the scent a couple of times around Beatriz. This miraculous event reaffirmed for me that Mary was indeed by our side, although we could not see Her. Having the presence of Mary in my house increased my devotion for Her tremendously.

Several years went by, and many other authors populated my list. Neal Donald Walsh, Wayne Dyer, Tony de Mello, Marianne Williamson, Miguel Ruiz, and visionaries, like Maria Valtorta, contributed many of the missing jigsaw pieces. I also read Carlos Castaneda, Dolores Cannon, and books on Edgar Cayce's channels with much interest. There are many people on Earth today who channel messages of Mary. However, there are as many different stories as there are authors writing them.

By 2007, it became evident to me that there was a need for a new book on Mary. There was a lot of information about Jesus and His life, but when it came to Mary, there was so much confusing information. We needed a book that would synthesize all this information, without a dogmatic focus, that would appeal to all peoples of all religious background...and I wanted to write it.

Mary's life is obscure because when the Christian church was organizing itself, Her story became entrapped by men's egos and politics. At the time of Jesus and Mary, women were second-class citizens, with many obligations and few privileges. Men took a commanding role in the nascent Christian church, and there was no place for a woman in a protagonist role. Mary's legacy survived through the faithful, as evidenced by the architectural works dedicated to Her and the paintings done of Her. But later on She was placed in a closet and forgotten. It is only in the last 250 years that we see Her coming back with force.

In understanding the role of Mary in history, we have to go to the Bible for reference because She was created since the beginning of time.

Her coming was prepared for and anticipated for many generations because She would bear the Son of God. The Bible says that God created everything, including Adam and Eve, the first humans to inhabit the newly created Earth, and He gave them the Garden of Eden where Adam and Eve would get all they needed to live and multiply.

I have had trouble with this Genesis story. Perhaps you are like me; our rational minds have difficulty grasping concepts that are not logic-based. Is it a fictitious story, or did this really happen? Is it just a representation of events, and the writers of the time decorated the story in this way? I do not know. But let's give ourselves the chance to explore and to find how this story fits with the theme of this book.

God gave Adam and Eve *free will*, but asked of them only one thing —*obedience*. As Genesis describes the creation of Adam and Eve, it is explained that these first humans were created in the "image and likeness" of God.

> And God said, Let us make man in our image, after our likeness: and let them have dominion over the fish of the sea, and over the fowl of the air, and over the cattle, and over all the earth, and over every creeping thing that creepeth upon the earth. [Genesis 1:26]

God blessed them, saying: 'Be fruitful, multiply, fill the earth and subdue it.' God also said: 'Look, to you I give all the seed-bearing plants everywhere on the surface of the earth, and all the trees with seed-bearing fruit; this will be your food.' [Genesis 1:28-29 NJB[1]] God then created the trees, with two very special trees among them: The tree of life and the tree of knowledge of good and evil.

> And the LORD God planted a garden eastward in Eden; and there he put the man whom he had formed. And out of the ground

1 Scripture taken from the *New Jerusalem Bible* (NJB). Copyright © 1985 by Darton, Longman & Todd, Ltd. and Doubleday, a division of Bantam Doubleday Dell Publishing Group Inc. Quotes and references from this book are indicated as [vers #, NJB].

made the LORD God to grow every tree that is pleasant to the sight, and good for food; the tree of life also in the midst of the garden, and the tree of knowledge of good and evil. [Genesis 2:8–9]

So Adam and Eve were very gifted, or "graced," and one of these gifts was eternal life, represented by the tree of life in the middle of the garden. In this newly created world, the polarity of good and evil had to be present for free will to operate, which was provided in the tree of knowledge of good and evil. Imperfect Adam's and Eve's roles in this creation of God's was to pursue the ultimate perfection of God. They had to be *obedient* to God, while exercising their free will in the earthly realm, and not fall pray to the temptations of evil, which were present on Earth.

And the LORD God took the man, and put him into the garden of Eden to dress it and to keep it. And the LORD God commanded the man, saying, Of every tree of the garden thou mayest freely eat: But of the tree of the knowledge of good and evil, thou shalt not eat of it: for in the day that thou eatest thereof thou shalt surely die. [Genesis 2:15–17]

Interestingly, in addition to having access to eternal life and free will, God had given Adam and Eve other gifts that to us now would look supernatural. For instance, we know Eve could bear children without pain, something women cannot do today. We know that although they wore no garments over their physical bodies, they did not feel shame or embarrassment over their exposed nakedness, which to me implies that their bodies were probably highly energetic and bright, like Jesus' body in the transfiguration.

And they were both naked, the man and his wife, and were not ashamed. [Genesis 2:25]

This means Adam and Eve in their perfect purity could not see anything shameful in their bodies. Adam and Eve also did not have to work laboriously to earn a living like most of us have to do today, because they had the Garden of Eden at their disposal, with all sorts of plentiful sources of food.

According to Genesis, shortly after Eve was created, "The Fall" took place. Eve was tempted by the snake to eat the fruit from the forbidden tree, the tree of knowledge of good and evil. She falls prey to the temptation of evil, represented by the snake, and through her faculty of free will decides to *disobey* God. She is convinced by the snake that she does not have to subject herself to God, that once she eats the fruit she will be like God. Pride in action.

> And the serpent said unto the woman, Ye shall not surely die: For God doth know that in the day ye eat thereof, then your eyes shall be opened, and ye shall be as gods, knowing good and evil. [Genesis 3:4-5]

Eve follows the snake's advice and eats the forbidden fruit, becoming the first to *disobey* God. She then convinces Adam to eat the forbidden fruit, and he falls into the trap, disobeying God as well.

> And when the woman saw that the tree was good for food, and that it was pleasant to the eyes, and a tree to be desired to make one wise, she took of the fruit thereof, and did eat, and gave also unto her husband with her; and he did eat. [Genesis 3:6]

As soon as both had eaten the forbidden fruit Adam and Eve lost some of the wonderful gifts, or graces, granted initially by God. First, Eve will no longer bear children without pain.

> Unto the woman he said, I will greatly multiply thy sorrow and thy conception; in sorrow thou shalt bring forth children; and thy desire shall be to thy husband, and he shall rule over thee. [Genesis 3:16]

Adam would have to labor hard to procure food for them. They would no longer be able to simply procure food from the Garden of Eden.

> And unto Adam he said, Because thou hast hearkened unto the voice of thy wife, and hast eaten of the tree, of which I commanded thee, saying, Thou shalt not eat of it: cursed is the ground for thy sake; in sorrow shalt thou eat of it all the days of thy life; Thorns also and thistles shall it bring forth to thee; and thou shalt eat the herb of the field; In the sweat of thy face shalt thou eat bread, till thou return unto the ground; for out of it wast thou taken: for dust thou art, and unto dust shalt thou return. [Genesis 3:17-19]

They also suddenly became aware of their nakedness and felt shame, needing to quickly cover themselves up. Adam and Eve, because of their curiosity, lost their purity, their innocence, which gave rise to ego, to the concept of "I" separate from God, different from the original concept that "we are all one."

> And the eyes of them both were opened, and they knew that they were naked; and they sewed fig leaves together, and made themselves aprons. [Genesis 3:7]

> Also for Adam and his wife the LORD God made tunics of skin, and clothed them. [Genesis 3:21]

God then expelled them from the Garden of Eden, from Paradise, taking away from them eternal life, because He knew they would now sin. He knew that through free will, mankind had chosen a destiny that would bring much pain and sorrow upon them. By not allowing Adam and Eve access to the tree of life, God made sure this pain and sorrow would not be eternal.

> And the LORD God said, Behold, the man is become as one of us, to know good and evil: and now, lest he put forth his hand,

> and take also of the tree of life, and eat, and live for ever: Therefore the LORD God sent him forth from the garden of Eden, to till the ground from whence he was taken. [Genesis 3:22-23]

The original sin committed first by Eve and then by Adam, is the *disobedience* of God, which immediately led to their separation from God and *reduced the human race to a lesser expression of our human potentiality as created by God.* They both "fell" from the grace of God.

The reason I highlight Eve as the first sinner is because it is relevant to the role that Mary will play later on in history. When God says, "...man has become like one of us in knowing good from evil," it is implied that as long as man stayed obedient to God, he was to be spared the knowledge of evil. So although free will was part of man from the beginning, evil in itself was not. Suffering could have been avoided had Adam and Eve followed God's instructions by using their free will wisely.

I had heard the story of Adam and Eve before, but I had never read Genesis or inquired more about it. I had discarded this story as a fable, therefore not worth further consideration. But I now find it most intriguing, because here we have two human beings who were born in what modern terms could be described as "enlightenment," who then lost their enlightenment. What can we learn from them?

Over the last several years, I, for one, have been pursuing my own enlightenment. For me enlightenment means being once again full of grace; reaching the understanding of God, where as human beings we no longer suffer and can transcend to higher vibrating planes. Enlightenment for me does not mean a rejection of scripture or religious faith, although I fully respect other traditions that prefer a path of faith based solely on reason. I have found that reason alone does not work for me. I have, however, discovered elements in these "non-religious" paths that have indeed helped me, like meditation and Reiki, which is an Eastern tradition that uses laying of hands for healing.

If Adam and Eve lost their enlightenment when they separated from God, when they disobeyed God, then, if we reverse the behavior, we should be able to find enlightenment again. If we become *obedient* to God's will, we should be able to earn back the lost graces and find enlightenment. A very interesting thought, don't you think? The most popular Christian prayer is the Our Father. In its fifth verse it says, "Thy will be done." But how do we find out what is God's will in our lives?

We shall be exploring these thoughts further in this book, as they relate to the story of Mary. In my personal life I have found a way to identify God's will for me, and I will share what I have done to be as obedient as I can. We shall also see that Mary and Jesus came to undo Eve and Adam's original sin of disobedience and that they established the path so that humankind could find its way to enlightenment. So that you, dear reader, can find a way back home. A way back to Paradise.

Not only did humans fall, but the angels also fell. The fall of the angels also had important consequences for mankind. For one thing, Eve might not have been tempted by the snake, which embodies the evil nature of the fallen angels, with Lucifer at its culprit. We shall review this part of the creation story in the visions and writings of two women: Maria Valtorta and Anne Catherine Emmerich.

Maria Valtorta was born in 1897 in Caserta, Italy, and lived until 1961, dying at the age of sixty-five, making her a fairly recent mystic. Maria Valtorta was a hospital nurse when she had an accident that left her confined to a bed for the rest of her life. In her bed, between 1943 and 1953, she filled almost fifteen thousand handwritten pages about various biblical events. She wrote all these pages out of divine inspiration, receiving the information directly from Mary or Jesus and other biblical characters, and she never corrected any of her fifteen thousand handwritten pages.

Sometimes information was dictated to her. Other times she had visions, as if she were actually witnessing the events. Maria Valtorta declared, "I can affirm that I have had no human source to be able to know what I write, and what, even while writing, I often do not understand." In some of her writings, she referred to historical events and to geographical locations that were unknown to her; with subsequent verification, they were confirmed to be correct. Pope Pius XII said of Maria Valtorta's writings: *"Publish this work as it is. There is no need to give an opinion about its origin, whether it be extraordinary or not. Who reads it, will understand."* [His Holiness Pope Pius XII, Osservatore Romano, February 26, 1948]

Maria Valtorta's writings indicate that when all things were created, not just humans were created, but also angels. Humans were placed in the Garden of Eden and angels were placed in Angel's Paradise, also called Heaven. Angels and humans were created to live in love and friendship with God. The angel's test consisted of accepting the revelation that at some point in time, the divine Word would take flesh as a human being. The Word was God's First Eternal Thought, or the concept of God's Son. The test for humans consisted of obedience, of abstaining from eating the fruit of the forbidden tree.[2]

But both angels and humans failed their tests, thus falling from His grace. A group of angels, with Lucifer at its head, driven by pride, did not welcome God's Word incarnating as a human instead of assuming an angel nature, and they refused to worship Him. Because of this they were driven out of Heaven by God, into Hell. The remaining angels were troubled, discouraged, and uncertain. They felt lost and without hope. If the fallen angels had succumbed to pride, what would they do to remain in their purity, honoring God, and not also fall?

Anne Catherine Emmerich records similar events. A German Roman Catholic nun, mystic, and visionary, she lived from 1774 to 1824. Anne Catherine Emmerich's visions are vivid recollections of Mary's and Jesus' lives as if she were actually present in the places and times when the events occurred. In 2003, actor Mel Gibson brought Anne Catherine Emmerich's visions to prominence when he used them as an additional source for his movie *The Passion of the Christ.*

Anne Catherine Emmerich had visions since she was a child. She would correct, or complement, her religion teachers, based on the facts

---

2 *The Book of Azariah* by Maria Valtorta, page 280

that she had seen in her visions. She tells that at the time, she thought everyone had the same visions, and thus she talked about them. But she quickly discovered this was not the case and usually led to trouble, so she started keeping the visions to herself.

In 1813, she was confined to bed, and stigmata appeared on her body. The stigmata were wounds in the places where Jesus Christ had received His crucifixion wounds. During the last twelve years of her life, she could eat no food except the Holy Communion, nor take any drink but water. The priests and physicians examined her stigmata wounds and found them to be genuine and confirmed she was living exclusively on the Communion. Anne Catherine Emmerich's detailed descriptions of the place where Mary died helped archeologists find it. On October 3, 2004, Anne Catherine Emmerich was beatified by Pope John Paul II.

Anne Catherine Emmerich explains that man was created to fill the gap left by the fallen angels in heaven. She explains how Adam received a Blessing from God, in the shape of a bean, which was actually embedded in Adam's body. This Blessing contained the Word, or the Eternal Thought of God, from which Christ was to be born. Because of the Fall, this Blessing was removed from Adam. [*The Lowly*, I, pages 2–4][3]

Anne Catherine Emmerich also explains that the fallen angels, headed by Lucifer, separated from the other angels in Heaven because of pride. From her visions, she describes a large resplendent globe of light shining like a sun. Below this globe floated concentric circles, where the choirs of good angels resided, forming a smaller sphere. These had been born out of love from the large globe sun.

Suddenly, she saw a group of these angels become separate from the good angels and concentrate in another disc, but this time it was dark and much smaller than the sphere from which they had fallen. She explains that the reason why the angels fell was that they were rapt in

---

3 *The Lowly Life and Bitter Passion Of Our Lord Jesus Christ And His Blessed Mother; Together With The Mysteries Of The Old Testament* (1914) of Anne Catherine Emmerich is composed of four volumes in its English version. Quotes and references to these book are indicated as [*The Lowly*, Volume #, page XX].

the contemplation of their own beauty, complacent in the self.

Returning to Maria Valtorta's vision: when the good angels were desperate and out of hope, God quickly reacted and showed them Mary, also in God's Eternal Thought, which made them rejoice and celebrate, because there was a way out of the problem. The angels understood that God's plan would triumph in the end, and good would defeat evil.

Maria Valtorta records what actually happened according to the voice of one of the good angels, Azariah.[4] When Azariah speaks of the first revelation of Eternal Thought, he is referring to the incarnation of the divine Word—Christ. When he refers to the second revelation of Eternal Thought, he is referring to Mary.

> And if through the knowledge of the first [Eternal Thought] there came Disorder, created by the proud [angels], who did not want to adore the Divine Word, through knowledge of the second [Eternal Thought] the peace which had been disturbed returned to us.
>
> We saw Mary in God's Eternal Thought. Seeing Her and possessing that wisdom, which is comfort, security, and peace, was one and the same thing. We saluted our future Queen with song of our Light and contemplated Her gratuitous and voluntary perfections. Oh, the beauty of that moment in which, for the comfort of his angels, the Eternal presented to them the jewel of his Love and Power! And we saw Her, so humble as to make up by Herself alone for all creaturely pride.
>
> From then on She was our teacher in not turning gifts into an instrument of ruin. Not her corporeal effigy, but her spirituality spoke to us wordlessly, and we were preserved from every thought of pride by having contemplated for an instant, in the Thought of God, the Most Humble One. For ages and ages we worked in the sweetness of that radiant revelation. For ages and ages, through eternity, we have rejoiced and rejoice and shall rejoice in possessing Her whom we contemplated spiritually. The Joy of God is our joy, and

---

4 Azariah is Archangel Rafael, as explained in the Bible in Tobit 5:4 & 5:13

we keep ourselves in his Light so as to be penetrated with it and to give joy and glory to Him who created us. [*The Book of Azariah*, page 281]

Mary was announced by God to the good angels, allowing them to rejoice, giving them the knowledge that after the Fall of angels and man, there was still hope of God's creation straightening its path. The equivalent image in Genesis would be when God shows Mary crushing the snake with Her foot. This is the origin of the image of Mary stepping over the serpent as a sign of the triumph of good over evil.

> I will put enmities between you [the serpent] and the Woman, and your seed and Her seed: She shall crush your head, and you shall lie in wait for Her heel. [Genesis 3:15 NJB]

I can only wonder if God had anticipated the angel's Fall and human's Fall when He envisioned Mary, or whether He created Mary assuming neither angels nor humans would fall. Either way, it is clear that Mary was announced to the angels after the angel's Fall and after human's Fall and was God's way of repairing the damage done by Lucifer and Eve. Therefore, Mary has existed in God's plan since the very beginning of time.

In another conversation recorded by Maria Valtorta, of Jesus with the disciples, He makes a reference to Mary existing since the beginning of time.

> "The soul of My Mother was thought by God *from everlasting.* It is therefore eternal in beauty, in which God poured every perfection to receive delight and comfort from it." [*The Poem*, III, 402][5]

Now here is the key. If Mary has existed since the beginning of time, then there must be a plan that encompasses how Mary is to come

5 *The Poem of the Man God* by Maria Valtorta is composed of five volumes in its English version. Quotes and references from these books are indicated as [*The Poem*, Volume #, page xx].

to life, to incarnate. I think that this time God wanted to make sure that He got it right, so He did not take any shortcuts. It took many centuries and many generations for Mary to walk the Earth after Adam and Eve. In my opinion, all these generations were necessary to purify the human race and allow for Mary to be born.

We will review some critical chapters of the history of these generations and what was written in the old books of the Bible to testify to this effect. As we shall discover, the issue of *obedience* to God was key throughout history. Had mankind *obeyed* God earlier, perhaps Mary would have come earlier, but it took many thousands of years and many generations for mankind to evolve and finally bring forth people with sufficient purity of heart to birth Mary.

We shall also review the role of Mary in the end of time. If She existed since the beginning of time, it would only make sense that She will also have a protagonist role at the end of times, whenever this may be. Which should make you wonder then why so many apparitions of Mary have occurred in recent years. Could it be that She is preparing the way once more for our salvation?

Chapter 2

The Mysterious Blessing and God's Will

The last chapter explained that Mary has existed in God's plan since the beginning of time and that Adam and Eve, through their disobedience, made human beings lose much of our likeness to God and reduced us to a much lower expression than our original blueprint. We will now review how God is to repair the damage done by Adam and Eve, providing an opportunity for mankind to regain some of its purity. We'll see how God paved the way for Mary's birth through the patriarchs.

After Adam and Eve left Paradise, they had to live what we now consider normal human lives, with all life's typical joys and frustrations. They had many children; the first were Cain and Abel, the two brothers of the famous story. Out of jealousy, Cain killed Abel, manifesting quickly the evil nature of the infant human race. Adam and Eve then had another child called Seth, through whom the patriarch lineage will follow. Seth lived for eight hundred and seventy years, quite a span in comparison with our current expectancies.

I counted nine generations between Seth and Noah. People at the time had children well into old age, so Earth was quickly being populated. It also seems that people continued in their sinful ways as the population was growing. Because of this, God decided to shorten the life span of man to one hundred and twenty years, something that did not happen immediately, but gradually, as we shall see later.

> And the LORD said, My spirit shall not always strive with man, for that he also is flesh: yet his days shall be an hundred and twenty years. [Genesis 6:3]

But reducing life span was not enough; God was so disgusted with the human race that he decided to send the great universal flood to wipe out mankind. He trusted Noah to preserve the human race and animal kingdom.

> And God saw that the wickedness of man was great in the earth, and that every imagination of the thoughts of his heart was only evil continually. And it repented the LORD that he had made man on the earth, and it grieved him at his heart. And the LORD said, I will destroy man whom I have created from the face of the earth; both man, and beast, and the creeping thing, and the fowls of the air; for it repenteth me that I have made them. But Noah found grace in the eyes of the LORD. [Genesis 6:5–8]

You know the rest of Noah's story. He built the ark following God's instructions, and he took with him his wife, his three sons—Shem, Ham, and Japheth—whom he had fathered when he was five hundred years old, and his son's wives. After the flood had subsided, they disembarked and started a new world order.

> And God blessed Noah and his sons, and said unto them, Be fruitful, and multiply, and replenish the earth. [Genesis 9:1]

> And the sons of Noah, that went forth of the ark, were Shem, and Ham, and Japheth: and Ham is the father of Canaan. These are the three sons of Noah: and of them was the whole earth overspread. [Genesis 9:18–19]

God then established a covenant with Noah and his sons. God said He would never again destroy all living things by the waters of a flood. But He also required them to obey two rules: they could not eat flesh with life, and they could not kill their fellow man. These simple requests required *obedience.*

The lineage of the patriarchs after the flood continued down through Shem. Nine generations after Shem—each living progressively shorter lives as decided by God—came Abram. His family was native to Ur but had moved to Haran, an ancient city of Mesopotamia, now in southeast Turkey.

As we can see, Abram, who later is called Abraham in the Bible, was a direct descendant of Noah. He was the first of the "chosen people;" the people who were to prepare the way for the coming of Mary. Abram was probably going about his normal business in Haran, the town where he lived, when he was approached by God one day. God asked Abram to leave Haran with his wife Sarai and go to Canaan.

> Now the LORD had said unto Abram, Get thee out of thy country, and from thy kindred, and from thy father's house, unto a land that I will shew thee: And I will make of thee a great nation, and I will bless thee, and make thy name great; and thou shalt be a blessing: [Genesis 12:1–2]

Abram took his wife and his nephew, along with their possessions, and headed to Canaan. This was around 1850 BC. I believe it must have been very difficult for Abram to do this. God had never spoken to him before; at the time man worshiped many gods and had no concept of a single God. How could he know if it was truly God and not his imagination talking to him?

Haven't we all been in this situation, when we hear a voice in our hearts ask us to do something? Our rational minds, quick to analyze the situation, will convince us that it is not God talking to us, but our imaginations. Then we disregard the event and forget about it. This has happened to me many times, but in recent years, I have learned to listen more to my heart and to be attentive and responsive to its signals.

In November 2006, Beatriz and I went to a beautiful resort in Sedona, Arizona, for five days. Sedona is one of the most beautiful places on earth. It is situated in the northern part of Arizona, at an altitude of four thousand five hundred feet above sea level. It is quite green, and in winter it snows several times. Its major attributes are rock formations, which decorate the landscape with red and orange colors. Sunsets in Sedona are beautiful, because the sun will illuminate the rocks with new light every day, creating unusual colors.

By the end of our five-day stay, we were sad to have to leave. As we were waiting for the airplane in Phoenix airport to take the runway, I told Beatriz that I felt I was leaving a place that was dear to my heart. I had not experienced this feeling in my home city of Miami or in any of the other places where I had lived before that. Interestingly, Beatriz felt the same way.

Beatriz and I talked about how nice it would be to live in Sedona, but we realized how big a change it would be in our lives. For one thing, I was heading an international company, which I had helped build. I had to travel to our overseas offices frequently. How would I continue to do my job working from Sedona, with the Phoenix airport almost two hours away? It did not seem feasible. We would also have to move the girls to different schools and leave all our friends.

But the calling in our hearts for Sedona grew stronger and stronger. We no longer wanted to stay in Miami. We had had our house for sale for several months in 2006, without any success. We wanted to move to another area in the city that would be closer to my office downtown. My commute to the office had doubled in time over the past several years because of the increasing city traffic. Our contract with the realtor was due to expire in a few weeks, but the house was not selling.

We decided that once the contract expired, we would list the house for sale by owner, and if the house sold, we would interpret this as a first step, a positive response from God and the universe to a future move to Sedona. There was still the major hurdle of my work to deal with, but we decided we would tackle one issue at the time.

The real estate contract expired, and two days later we received a call from a person interested in purchasing the house. They came to see the house, fell in love with it, and made us an offer we could not reject. Moreover, since we were now listing the house by owner, we were able to save on the commissions. We thought then that this quick response was a very strong sign that Sedona was a real possibility for us.

The next step was to get agreement from my business partners for me to work remotely. I promptly discussed this option with them, and, to my surprise, they were very supportive of my move. Shortly after this, I received a salary increase, so I guess my partners wanted to make sure I remained with the company while working out of Sedona. Now we knew that Sedona was going to become a reality.

What is interesting about this story is that God was speaking to us. He was speaking to us through our hearts. We could have chosen to ignore this and go about our normal business, but we did not. We not only listened, but we also put our minds and efforts to work to try to follow our hearts' advice.

In my experience, when doors are opening for you with ease, as with our move to Sedona, it means that the whole universe is conspiring to make this happen for you. God is moving the strings so that His will may be manifest in our lives. On the contrary, when doors remain shut for us, and, despite our best efforts, we cannot move forward, it is because we are trying to move in a direction that is not God's will for us. Does this sound familiar? It certainly does to me.

What would have happened if Abram had not followed God's request and instead stayed in the comfort of his well-known life in Haran? We do not really know, but just maybe I would not have written this book, and you would not be reading it.

The probability of God appearing and just telling us what we need to do is very small, if not practically impossible for most of us. So how can we discover what God's will is in our lives? Well, one way is to listen to what our hearts are saying through the practice of meditation and prayer. You will read more about this in subsequent chapters.

Sometime later, when Abram was already in Canaan territory, there was a famine in the country, and Abram had to move to Egypt with his family to survive the severe famine. Sarai, Abram's wife, was a very beautiful woman, and the Pharaoh noticed her. To make a long story short, the Pharaoh helped Abram and Sarai, and they became very wealthy in Egypt. After some time, Abram and Sarai returned home to Canaan, but they had not had any children.

When Abram was ninety-nine years old, God appeared again and established His covenant with him. "Live in my presence, be perfect," he said. [Genesis 17:1 NJB] God asked him to change his name to Abraham and Sarai to Sarah. He promised him he would have a son from Sarah. But Abraham did not believe this, because Sarah was also old and barren.

> As for me, behold, my covenant is with thee, and thou shalt be a father of many nations. Neither shall thy name any more be called Abram, but thy name shall be Abraham; for a father of many nations have I made thee. And I will make thee exceeding fruitful, and I will make nations of thee, and kings shall come out of thee. [Genesis 17:4–6]

> And I will bless her, and give thee a son also of her: yea, I will bless her, and she shall be a mother of nations; kings of people shall be of her. Then Abraham fell upon his face, and laughed, and said in his heart, Shall a child be born unto him that is an hundred years old? and shall Sarah, that is ninety years old, bear? [Genesis 17:16–17]

God continued and explained He would maintain His covenant with him, to be Abrahams' God and the God of his descendants in perpetuity. He told Abraham that He was instituting the circumcision on all males as a sign of the covenant. Abraham followed God's instruction, and his entire household, including himself, was circumcised.

Later God appeared to Abraham again, this time as three men, while he was sitting in front of his tent. God reiterated his earlier promise that there would be a child born to him and Sarah and that the child must be named Isaac. He then said that He would come back the following year; by then Sarah would already have had the child. Sarah laughed within herself, saying, "After I am waxed old shall I have pleasure, my lord being old also?" [Genesis 18:12] God replies to Abraham that Sarah's laughter is unjustified, because nothing is impossible for God.

Anne Catherine Emmerich offers a similar version of these events in her visions. Abraham was sitting in front of his tent under a large tree, next to his altar, immersed in prayer, when he saw in a sunbeam in the sky an announcement of the coming of three men. Abraham stood and sacrificed a lamb in the altar in thankful prayer. Before the sacrifice was complete, three angels appeared on the road headed in his direction. Abraham hurried to meet them, bowed before them, and led them to his tent and the altar.

At the altar, the angels commanded Abraham to kneel. The first angel announced to Abraham that God would bring "an immaculate maiden who, while remaining an inviolate virgin, should be the mother of the Redeemer." The angel also announced to him that Abraham was now going to receive from them what Adam had lost through sin.

The angel made him eat a small portion of a shining object and drink a luminous fluid out of a little cup. He then blessed him with his right hand, making three straight lines that met below the breast: one coming down from Abraham's forehead, another from the right shoulder and another from the left shoulder. Then, the angel held something with both hands, "like a luminous cloud," and brought it towards Abraham's breast, until it entered him. This was the same Blessing that had been removed from Adam.

The second angel then told Abraham that he should impart the blessing to Sarah's first-born in the same way that he had received the blessing. Notice the terminology, although Sarah would only have one son, the angel still referred to him as the first-born. This will be relevant later on. He also told him that his grandson Jacob would be the father of twelve sons, from whom twelve tribes would spring.

The third angel told Abraham that Sarah's first-born should be called Isaac. When this third angel is speaking to Abram, Sarah hears that she will bear a son and cannot but laugh at the idea that at her old age she would be able to conceive a child.

Sarah did indeed conceive and give birth to a child as God had foretold, and he was called Isaac. And then comes perhaps one of the most difficult parts of the Bible: when God puts Abraham to the test and asks him to sacrifice Isaac.

> And he said, Take now thy son, thine only son Isaac, whom thou lovest, and get thee into the land of Moriah; and offer him there for a burnt offering upon one of the mountains which I will tell thee of. [Genesis 22:2]

In the absence of the earlier background about the role of *obedience*, this request is an absolute monstrosity. How could God even ask for such a thing? But God wanted to see if Abraham was indeed going to be *obedient*. From Abraham were to descend generations upon generations that would eventually bring forth Mary. If Abraham was not going to be *obedient* to the will of God, then the whole plan would fail.

The story is that Abraham, in perfect *obedience*, did indeed intend to carry out God's instructions. At the last minute, the angel of God appeared again and said, "Lay not thine hand upon the lad, neither do thou any thing unto him: for now I know that thou fearest God, seeing thou hast not withheld thy son, thine only son from me." [Genesis 22:12] Then God went on to say:

> By myself have I sworn, saith the LORD, for because thou hast done this thing, and hast not withheld thy son, thine only son: That in blessing I will bless thee, and in multiplying I will multiply thy seed as the stars of the heaven, and as the sand which is upon the sea shore; and thy seed shall possess the gate of his enemies; And in thy seed shall all the nations of the earth be blessed; because thou hast obeyed my voice. [Genesis 22:16-18]

The reappearance of the term *obedience* is important here and will continue to be a recurring theme with the patriarchs. God needed the human race to purify itself, and for this He needed *obedience*. And what is *obedience* if not just having the wisdom to understand what God's will is in our lives and then having the courage to follow it? But how do we find out what God's will is in our lives?

Finding God's Will in Silence

This is probably one of the most difficult things for us to accomplish. Following God's will is a way for us to go back to Paradise, to find enlightenment. It is a difficult thing to do because we don't always know what God's will is in our lives; thus, how can we direct our lives in an unknown direction? This is a type of "chicken and egg" question; which came first? Mary in Her messages from Medjugorje is constantly asking us to seek God's will.

> Mary's Message of April 25, 2008, from Medjugorje: "Dear children! ... *Seek God's will* and do good to those whom God has put on your way, and be light and joy. Thank you for having responded to my call." [http://www.medjugorje.org]

Following God's will is like being in a boat in the middle of the ocean, where God is in control of the tiller that steers the boat and you are in control of the oars. The boat will not move forward if you do not row. But if you row, you don't know in which direction the boat will move, because it is God who has control. What comes first: knowing the direction or rowing? The chicken or the egg? I recommend that you never stop rowing, even if you do not know where you are going. It is a way to express trust in God and a demonstration that you will work hard at following God's will.

This may sound silly at first, but this is what has worked best in my life. Many times I have been faced with situations that seem unfavorable at first or where the direction was not clear. Only because I have kept going have things worked out for the better later on. God always knows what is best for us, and we have to trust in His better judgment. So keep rowing and asking God to show you the way. Never stop, because that disrupts the flow of universal abundance in your life.

How do we find silence to listen to God in our hearts? Here is what I did: I turned off as much noise in my life as I could. I stopped the newspaper subscriptions that were invading my life with mostly useless, negative information, to rid myself of the yoke of the news, of the "need to be informed." My mother would often criticize me because I would become ignorant of the world and its events. But informed for what purpose? Even in business, I confirmed that I could do very well without the flood of sensationalistic news that surrounds our lives.

> Mary's Message of July 25, 2006, from Medjugorje: "Dear children! At this time, do not only think of rest for your body but, little children, seek time also for the soul. In *silence* may the Holy Spirit speak to you and permit Him to convert and change you. I am with you and before God I intercede for each of you..." [www.medjugorje.org]

I drastically reduced my time in front of the television and stopped watching sports events that drained so many hours from my life. I also drastically reduced the amount of time I listened to music, despite my love of music, and I opted to stay away from iPods and similar devices that wire your brain. The time I gained from all of this was productively used to read about Mary, Jesus, and the saints or the Bible, which served a much higher purpose: my return to God.

> Mary's Message of May 25, 2007, from Medjugorje: "Dear children! Pray with me to the Holy Spirit for Him to lead you in the search of *God's will* on the way of your holiness. And you, who are far from prayer, convert and, in the *silence of your heart*, seek salvation for your soul and nurture it with prayer..." [www.medjugorje.org]

Kierkegaard, the nineteenth-century Danish philosopher and theologian, one of the foremost Christian minds, said that if he could prescribe only one remedy for all the ills of the modern world, he would prescribe silence. Even if the word of God was proclaimed again, it would not be heard because there is so much noise.

Back in 2002, the company I was working for became insolvent and could not continue to pay my salary. I felt in my heart that God wanted me to stay there, so I did, despite having no stock participation as incentive. The company had fallen into major debt and was in the middle of a major legal battle between the venture capital holders of the majority of the stock and the original founders. All rational analysis would have pointed towards leaving this job. Despite the hardships brought to my family, I stayed in this situation for nine months, only to later become the owner of a major portion of the stock of this company. When I left the CEO position of the company in 2008, the value of my stock paid out several times my nine-month investment at no salary. This is how God does His work in our lives.

Abraham lived until he was one hundred and seventy-five years. [Genesis 25-7] From Abraham and Sarah's son, Isaac, the patriarch lineage continued with two twins: Esau and Jacob, Jacob being the one that received the Blessing from Isaac. From Jacob, whose name was changed by God to Israel [Genesis 35:10], were then born twelve sons from two wives. One night when Jacob was returning to Canaan, the angel of God wrestled with him, and as Anne Catherine Emmerich explains, his Blessing was removed by God. Let's see what the Bible says about this:

> And when he saw that he prevailed not against him, he touched the hollow of his thigh; and the hollow of Jacob's thigh was out of joint, as he wrestled with him. And he said, Let me go, for the day breaketh. And he said, I will not let thee go, except thou bless me. And he said unto him, What is thy name? And he said, Jacob. And he said, Thy name shall be called no more Jacob, but Israel: for as a

> prince hast thou power with God and with men, and hast prevailed. [Genesis 32:25-28]

Jacob understood that the Blessing had been removed from his body. That is why Jacob did not want to let go until he was blessed. The angel of God, before leaving, did bless him, but he did not reinstate the Blessing that contained the Eternal Thought to Jacob.

I believe the Blessing was removed from Jacob because the twelve tribes of Israel had already been created in Jacob's twelve sons. The Blessing was to belong to the entire nation of Israel and not just to one tribe. Later on, we shall see how the Blessing will find its permanent home in the Ark of the Covenant that Moses had to build.

All of Jacob's descendents end up in Egypt, with Joseph, Jacob's favorite son, taking the protagonist role in the biblical story. Joseph is the envy of his brothers. Because of this, Joseph is betrayed by his brothers and sold as a slave to a trading caravan and taken to Egypt, where he lives the rest of his life.

Anne Catherine explains that Joseph arrived in Egypt, and while in prison he received the Blessing from an angel of God, the same Blessing that had been removed from Jacob. She explains that the Blessing gave Abraham, Isaac, and Jacob more strength in their right sides than in their left. There was a fullness, or swelling, in that side, which is where the Blessing resided, although it was not noticeable because they wore loose clothing.

Through his wisdom and ability to interpret dreams, a skill attributable to carrying the Blessing, Joseph gained the favor of the Pharaoh and became an important person in Egypt. Anne Catherine explains that in Egypt Joseph's name was Osiris, same as one of the deities that the Egyptians worshiped.

As years went by, the Israelites, as they are now called, prospered and multiplied, becoming numerous and powerful. The Pharaoh of Egypt, seeing that the Israelites posed a threat to his kingdom, became concerned and put them into forced labor. This did not stop the growth of the Israelites, so the Pharaoh then ordered the murder of all newborn Israelite boys.

This is how the story of Moses begins. Moses was the son of a man who descended from Levi, who was one of Jacob's sons. Soon after he was born, his mother placed him in a papyrus basket among the reeds at the river's edge. When the Pharaoh's daughter went down to bathe in the river, she noticed the basket among the reeds and recovered it. Feeling sorry for the child, she decided to keep him, and she named him Moses.

Moses grew up under the protection of the Pharaoh's daughter. But one day, when he was already a grown man [Exodus 2:11], he defended an Israelite who was being hit by an Egyptian and ended up killing the Egyptian. The Pharaoh heard of this and tried to put Moses to death, but Moses was able to escape before they could capture him.

Moses fled Egypt to the Midianite territory, where he settled, married, and had a child. During this period, the Israelites continued in slavery, crying out for God's help. God, remembering his covenant with Abraham, Isaac, and Jacob, heard the Israelite's cry for help and appeared to Moses in the famous burning bush.

During this encounter with God, Moses received the instructions for his mission to free the Israelites and take them out of Egypt and into the Promised Land. The conversation between Moses and God in Exodus is quite long. Moses first showed his unbelief and then unsuccessfully tried to get out of the job God was sending his way. But God provided sufficient proof of his powers and convinced Moses to do it. God made sure that Moses took a staff, a long wooden stick, with which he would later perform the miracles that astonished everyone in Egypt.

Moses, *obediently*, returns to Egypt with his brother Aaron and his wife and son, and they talked to the Israelites about what God had told Moses. He also talked to the Pharaoh, but the Pharaoh, instead of listening, made the Israelites labor more difficult. So Moses started to perform the miracles anticipated by God. He transformed his staff into a snake, and then he used his staff to convert the waters of the river into blood, killing all fish and making the river stink.

This was the first of the ten plagues that Moses, under the command of God, unfolded for the Pharaoh. Next came the frogs that invaded the land, the mosquitoes, the horseflies, the death of all livestock belonging to the Egyptians, the boils (furuncles), the hail, the locust, the three-day darkness over all Egypt except where the Israelites lived, and the tenth: the death of all Egyptian first-born children.

Finally, after losing his first-born child, the Pharaoh lets Moses and the Israelites leave Egypt. The date of this event is around 1250 BC. In total, about six hundred thousand Israelites left [Exodus 12:37]; the total time they spent in Egypt was four hundred and thirty years. [Exodus 12:40]

Moses and the Israelites crossed the Red Sea in that famous episode of the opening of the waters. Once again, Moses used his staff to open the waters and crossed safely with all the six hundred thousand Israelites. The Pharaoh, who had changed his mind, sent the Egyptian soldiers in pursuit of the Israelites. But as the soldiers crossed the sea, they were swallowed by the closing waters.

Anne Catherine Emmerich explains that Moses took with him the remains of Joseph, who by then had died. Joseph's bones were an important relic for the Israelites, and they preserved them with great care, not knowing that the Blessing was still in them.

After crossing the Red Sea, one of the first things that God ordered Moses to do was to build the Ark of the Covenant and house in it the remains of Joseph, which still contained the Blessing. We shall learn more about the Ark of the Covenant and its whereabouts in the next chapter.

There are theories that Moses was not actually of Jewish descent, but that he was an Egyptian, related to the Thutmosis Pharaoh line. This theory is strongly rejected by Jewish scholars, because Moses is one of the main patriarchs of the Jewish faith. The Bible supports the Hebrew theory quite strongly, mentioning that he descended from the tribe of Levi, one of Jacob's sons.

Either way, Moses' role in the history of the Israelites was to save them from slavery in Egypt and to govern them until they reached the Promised Land and also to build the Ark of the Covenant and to place in it the Blessing that was in Joseph's bones, so that the Blessing would belong to the whole nation of Israel. The bloodline that Mary was to come from does not cross with Moses'. In fact, in the Bible there is no further reference to the son of Moses.

This historic review establishes that from the beginning of time, God created Mary in His infinite wisdom. There was a lineage of people who were chosen by God, with whom He communicated, out of which eventually Mary would be born. We discovered the Blessing, initially given to Adam but removed because of the Fall, that was reinstated with Abraham. Contained in this Blessing was the future salvation of mankind—God's Word, or God's Eternal Thoughts: Mary and Jesus.

Chapter 3

The Ark of the Covenant

One of the most intriguing historic artifacts of all time is probably the Ark of the Covenant, also called the Ark of the Testimony. If not the most intriguing, it stands right next to the Holy Grail in terms of power, mystery, and historic significance. I was happily surprised in my readings when I discovered that the Ark of Covenant was made to preserve the Blessing, which contained God's Word. It made complete sense that such a treasure would be preserved and passed on from generation to generation. An important piece of my puzzle had been found.

The Blessing that had been with Abraham, Isaac, Jacob, and Joseph would find its home in the Ark of the Covenant, until reaching Mary's father, Joachim. Once the Blessing was with Joachim, God manifested His Second Eternal Thought through the miraculous conception of Mary. She becomes the New Ark of the Covenant, because in Her womb was to reside The Word incarnate, the First Eternal Thought, the Son of God.

The Ark of the Covenant was a case, or chest, made by the Israelites during the time of Moses, while they were at Mount Sinai after the escape from Egypt, according to straightforward construction guidelines from God. In the Ark were to reside the tablets of the law, or

Ten Commandments, handed down to Moses directly by God and, more importantly, the Blessing that contained The Word, or Eternal Thoughts of God.

> And Moses came and told the people all the words of the LORD, and all the judgments: and all the people answered with one voice, and said, All the words which the LORD hath said will we do. And Moses wrote all the words of the LORD, and rose up early in the morning, and builded an altar under the hill, and twelve pillars, according to the twelve tribes of Israel. [Exodus 24:3–4]

Moses had some of his people offer burnt offerings and sacrifice bullocks to God. He took the Book of the Covenant, which he had just completed writing, and read it to the listening people, who then said, they would do everything that God had said; they would *obey*. Moses then took the blood of the sacrifice and sprinkled it over the people saying, "Behold the blood of the covenant, which the LORD hath made with you concerning all these words." [Exodus 28:8] During the time that Moses was up on Mount Sinai, God gave him detailed instructions on how to build the Ark that was to house the "Testimony," or the tablets of the law.

> And they shall make an ark of shittim wood: two cubits and a half shall be the length thereof, and a cubit and a half the breadth thereof, and a cubit and a half the height thereof. And thou shalt overlay it with pure gold, within and without shalt thou overlay it, and shalt make upon it a crown of gold round about. And thou shalt cast four rings of gold for it, and put them in the four corners thereof; and two rings shall be in the one side of it, and two rings in the other side of it. And thou shalt make staves of shittim wood, and overlay them with gold. And thou shalt put the staves into the rings by the sides of the ark, that the ark may be borne with them. The staves shall be in the rings of the ark: they shall not be taken from it. And thou shalt put into the ark the testimony which I shall give thee. [Exodus 25:10–16]

The Ark of the Covenant measured approximately four feet long, two and half feet wide, and two and half feet high and was made of wood and covered with gold. The top of the Ark held the "Mercy Seat," and on each of its sides were cherubim, or angels, with their wings in open position, like guardians.

> And thou shalt make a mercy seat of pure gold: two cubits and a half shall be the length thereof, and a cubit and a half the breadth thereof. And thou shalt make two cherubims of gold, of beaten work shalt thou make them, in the two ends of the mercy seat. And make one cherub on the one end, and the other cherub on the other end: even of the mercy seat shall ye make the cherubims on the two ends thereof. And the cherubims shall stretch forth their wings on high, covering the mercy seat with their wings, and their faces shall look one to another; toward the mercy seat shall the faces of the cherubims be. And thou shalt put the mercy seat above upon the ark; and in the ark thou shalt put the testimony that I shall give thee. And there I will meet with thee, and I will commune with thee from above the mercy seat, from between the two cherubims which are upon the ark of the testimony, of all things which I will give thee in commandment unto the children of Israel. [Exodus 25:17–22]

God also gave Moses detailed instruction on how to construct the place where the Ark was to be kept. In Exodus it is explained in detail how the "Tabernacle," also called the "Dwelling," or sanctuary, must be made, including frame, dimensions, and details of the rams' skins and linens to be used to cover it. The Israelites also had to build an altar, the table and lamps to be placed inside, and the "Tent of Meeting," or "Tent of Congregation," which was a space inside the Dwelling surrounded by a curtain, where the Ark was to be placed. This place, also referred to later as the "Holy of Holies," was where the Ark was kept and where God appeared regularly to communicate with Moses.

Moses' brother Aaron and Aaron's sons were selected by God to be the priests in His service [Exodus 28:1] and to serve in the newly created sanctuary. A long ceremony involving animal offerings to God took place to consecrate the priests and the altar. Then God instituted a daily offering on the altar of "two yearling male lambs each day in perpetuity."

> And there I will meet with the children of Israel, and the tabernacle shall be sanctified by my glory. And I will sanctify the tabernacle of the congregation, and the altar: I will sanctify also both Aaron and his sons, to minister to me in the priest's office. And I will dwell among the children of Israel, and will be their God. And they shall know that I am the LORD their God, that brought them forth out of the land of Egypt, that I may dwell among them: I am the LORD their God. [Exodus 29:43–46]

All these instructions were given to Moses during the forty days that he was on Mount Sinai. In the meantime, Moses' people had become anxious because Moses had not returned. They turned their backs on God and *disobeyed* Him, worshipping a golden calf they had built. Man's predisposition toward sin and against God continued since the time of Adam and Eve.

> And he gave unto Moses, when he had made an end of communing with him upon mount Sinai, two tables of testimony, tables of stone, written with the finger of God. [Exodus 31:18]

> And the LORD said unto Moses, Go, get thee down; for thy people, which thou broughtest out of the land of Egypt, have corrupted themselves: They have turned aside quickly out of the way which I commanded them: they have made them a molten calf, and have worshipped it, and have sacrificed thereunto, and said, These be thy gods, O Israel, which have brought thee up out of the land of Egypt. [Exodus 32:7–8]

Moses came down from Mount Sinai with the two tablets of the Testimony that had been given to him by God to find his people worshipping the golden calf. He was filled with such anger that he threw the tablets to the floor and crushed them. He then took several corrective measures to get his people back on track.

It is interesting that after all the miracles performed by God, including the ten plagues in Egypt, the magnificent splitting of the waters for the Israelites to escape Egypt, the manifestation of God on Mount Sinai, people were still obstinate and *disobeyed* God.

After thinking what I would have done in these circumstances, I came to the conclusion that I would not have been all that different. Think about this for a moment. Suppose that the adoration of a golden calf is equivalent to the adoration we have for the green dollar. Don't we put our desires for money ahead of anything else?

What about our desires for alcohol, or for drugs? These are called addictions. I propose to you that we humans have an addiction for money. We sometimes will hurt our friends and family in pursuit of money, just like an alcoholic may hurt his family when lost to alcohol. What about power? The pursuit of power is also an addiction. I know from personal experience.

When I graduated from university as a chemical engineer, I was still a simple young man, without preoccupations. I was the product of a "perfectly functional" family. My parents got along well together. I never saw them fighting. The relationship with my older sister and younger brother had always been very harmonious. I felt gifted by my many talents. It was easy for me to get good grades in school without much effort. I was good at sports and had lots of friends. I really had nothing to complain about in my life, except perhaps that I could not buy everything I wanted.

But when I boarded the train of the corporate world, things started to change. I began to adopt the corporate culture of my employer, a large multinational company. Slowly but surely, I was changing. A certain behavior was required to be successful in this company, and I learned it very well. Of course you had to be talented to climb the corporate ladder, and I had what was necessary for success.

After many years of hard work and long hours, I was finally in a position of power in the company. I was one of the top executives in one of the larger international subsidiaries in Latin America. I had one of those nice titles on my business card, and I was signing many of the checks that kept this company operating. It felt really good. I had many people reporting to me. For the first time, I started to notice that people were actually behaving differently with me. I started to receive more invitations and personal favors. I was tasting the drug of power for the first time and liking it. As time went by, the more I had this power drug, the more I wanted it.

You might be asking yourself, so what is wrong with this? What was wrong with me was that I was becoming someone else. I was losing my own identity. I no longer knew who I was. Power led to other behaviors I am not proud of. One of them was arrogance. I started to truly believe I was something else, that I was superior to most human beings around me. I felt I could undertake any business challenge and, if I applied myself enough, that I would successfully conquer it.

In my life back then, work, power, and money were replacing who I really was. As I explained earlier, I was not an active practitioner of any given faith. However, my parents surely taught me what good values were. Before entering the corporate world, I was a strong believer in God and had an open mind for God's miracles in my life. I felt much gratitude for all the talents He had given me. Now in the corporate world, my ego had replaced God. It was as if I had forgotten about God. I no longer needed Him.

Is this not then similar to what happened to the early Israelites? Your addiction may not be power, but perhaps vanity or the pursuit of fame, wanting to be a star or a millionaire. We all, to some degree, are ready to give up our God for some type of pleasure or something that feeds our ego. You see, ego wants to shut off God in your life. We are not all that different then, and things have not changed much since Moses time.

Returning to Moses' story: in one of his next encounters with God, he receives instructions to move to a new land, the Promised Land, which at the time was inhabited by the Canaanites, the Amorites, the Hittites, the Perizzites, the Hivites, and the Jebusites. God explains to Moses that he will protect the Israelites as they move into these lands. God also instructs Moses to carve two pieces of stone and ascend again to Mount Sinai, so the broken tablets of the Testimony can be recreated. Moses does just that; he takes the stones to God, who carves them again and returns them to Moses.

It took the Israelites one full year to build all the structures and elements of the Dwelling. Then Moses, following the divine commands given to him by God, placed the two tablets of the Testimony in the Ark. Immediately after that, a cloud covered the Tent of Meeting in the Dwelling.

> Then a cloud covered the tent of the congregation, and the glory of the LORD filled the tabernacle. And Moses was not able to enter into the tent of the congregation, because the cloud abode thereon, and the glory of the LORD filled the tabernacle. [Exodus 40:34–35]

God once more made a covenant with the Israelites to stay by their side, a covenant He had made many times before with Moses' ancestors, including Noah, Abraham, Isaac, and Jacob. Despite all of man's infidelities, God continued to support a specific group of people: not all people, just the Israelites, those of the lineage of the patriarchs.

God did this because He was paving the way for Mary. He selected a group of people, which He would coach and nurture, without taking from them their free will. These people, by following God's instructions, by being *obedient*, should be able to lead more holy lives.

He had them build the Ark of the Testimony to house and protect the Blessing, along with all the objects in the sanctuary, in such a way that they can carry it all with them along their journey. The rings of the Ark and similar rings on the furniture and altar were placed there to facilitate the transportation of the sanctuary as the Israelites marched to the Promised Land.

Anne Catherine Emmerich explains[1] that in the Ark were also placed relics of Jacob's and Joseph's family, the chalice and cup of the patriarchs, which belonged to Abraham, and later the rod of Aaron, Moses' brother and the first priest. She also explains that in the middle of the Ark was a small but unnoticeable door, by which the high priest when alone could take out the Blessing, or "Holy Thing" as she also calls it, for prophesying.

> It always seemed to me that all in the Ark of the Covenant was holy, that all our salvation was in it, as if rolled up in a ball, as if in a germ. The Holy Thing of the Ark was more mysterious than the Most Blessed Sacrament. [*The Lowly*, I, 112]

The presence of the Blessing was not known to all of the priests who were entrusted to care for the Ark. In fact, only a few, the chosen ones, through divine revelation, knew what it was and were able to use its incredible powers. This explains how later on, in Israelite history, some priests were able to prophesize for their kings with so much accuracy.

Once the Blessing was placed in the Ark of the Covenant, it belonged to the whole nation of Israel. Before, it had been carried by Abraham, Isaac, Jacob, and Joseph, as if belonging to just one family. Now it belonged to all the Israelites.

When God was present in the sanctuary housing the Ark, a cloud covered it and fire illuminated the inside of the Dwelling. When Moses went into the Tent of Meeting to converse with God, his face radiated a special kind of light when he emerged. This was so noticeable that he decided to start wearing a special veil over his face to cover the radiance it emanated.

Whenever the cloud rose from the Tent, the Israelites would break camp and continue their journey. Wherever the cloud halted, there the

---

1 *The Lowly*, page 110

Israelites would pitch camp. There they would remain for as long as the cloud rested on the Dwelling. The Israelites obediently pitched camp and lifted it many times during their journey. [Numbers 9:15]

Sometime in the second year after the exodus from Egypt, God assigned the Levites the important task of carrying and caring for the Dwelling and the Ark. The Levites, like Moses and Aaron, were the descendents of the tribe of Levi. Therefore, it was fitting over the next many centuries for the priests that were to care for the Ark to always be Levites.

Aaron was the first priest, appointed by God himself, and was later followed by his four sons. The first two died, consumed by fire when they offered an unauthorized sacrificial fire before the Ark. The Ark's transportation required special care, because no unauthorized person was to touch or see it; the penalty was death. Aside from Moses, Aaron and his sons were the only ones who could come close to the Ark.

It must have been a daunting task to take down the Dwelling and set it back up again every time they traveled. That is why the whole tribe of Levi was assigned this task. Sometimes they would camp in a place for just a few days, sometimes for a month, depending on God's will. Imagine doing this for over forty years, which is the period of time the Israelites marched through the desert.

At the end of the forty years, as Moses aged, he had to choose his successor. Moses chose Joshua, son of Nun, who had been assisting him inside the Tent and had served him since he was a boy. [Numbers 11:28] Joshua had the huge challenge of taking over after Moses, the man who had the privilege of speaking directly to God for over forty years, the man in charge of making sure that the behavior of the Israelites was in accordance to God's laws.

The rites and customs decreed by God and established by Moses had the purpose of keeping the Israelites close to God and helping them develop in holiness over the centuries. The Book of Leviticus in the Old Testament provides great detail about these rituals and the Law of Holiness. When you read Leviticus, you cannot but notice that many of the laws given to the Israelites by God had the purpose of keeping the Israelites healthy, through good hygiene practices as well as proper moral conduct. However, the paramount principle was to make sure the Israelites would serve God and no other.

My conclusion after reading all these laws is that the lifestyle of people at the time was in general terms very unhealthy and inappropriate for the development of a more pure human race. From poor eating habits, through sexual relations with animals, to the sacrifice of people, it was all pitifully unclean and unworthy. If we place ourselves in this context, we begin to understand God's relentless efforts to correct these ways of life and have humankind recognize its own superior human value.

Joshua led the Israelites across the Jordan and started conquering Canaan around 1210 BC, zealously protecting the Ark and the Dwelling, maintaining Moses' promises to God. The Ark was used to protect and defend the Israelites against its enemies and to help them conquer territories from the peoples that were occupying these lands. It seems that the Ark, containing its Blessing, had the power to amplify the intentions of the priest that invoked its powers. The waters of the Jordan River were separated and the walls of Jericho destroyed with the power of the Ark.

An important aspect of the Israelites moving into the new territories of the Promised Land centered around preserving their newly established religious practice. God had instructed Moses and Joshua that the Israelites were not to mix with the peoples of the conquered territories, particularly because religious practices not in accordance with theirs would infiltrate and weaken the recently established Israelite way of worshipping God.

> And he said, Behold, I make a covenant: before all thy people I will do marvels, such as have not been done in all the earth, nor in any nation: and all the people among which thou art shall see the work of the LORD: for it is a terrible thing that I will do with thee. Observe thou that which I command thee this day: behold, I drive out before thee the Amorite, and the Canaanite, and the Hittite, and the Perizzite, and the Hivite, and the Jebusite. Take heed to

> thyself, lest thou make a covenant with the inhabitants of the land whither thou goest, lest it be for a snare in the midst of thee: But ye shall destroy their altars, break their images, and cut down their groves: For thou shalt worship no other god: for the LORD, whose name is Jealous, is a jealous God: Lest thou make a covenant with the inhabitants of the land, and they go a whoring after their gods, and do sacrifice unto their gods, and one call thee, and thou eat of his sacrifice; And thou take of their daughters unto thy sons, and their daughters go a whoring after their gods, and make thy sons go a whoring after their gods. [Exodus 34:10–16]

God had been restraining His chosen people on a short leash for forty years to keep them from derailing, as the rest of mankind had been doing for centuries. His chosen people had to be protected from the rest to survive; otherwise they would just disappear as they melded with the rest of sinful mankind. God makes a reference to how people in Canaan sacrificed their own children to their gods. Talking about the Canaanite cults, He says:

> Thou shalt not do so unto the LORD thy God: for every abomination to the LORD, which he hateth, have they done unto their gods; for even their sons and their daughters they have burnt in the fire to their gods. [Deuteronomy 12:31]

This protection was with the purpose of assuring the survival of the chosen people who were to bring forth Mary, the mother of the Savior, and then in turn Jesus, the Son of God. It is not because the Israelites had earned particular favors from God. God says:

> Not for thy righteousness, or for the uprightness of thine heart, dost thou go to possess their land: but for the wickedness of these nations the LORD thy God doth drive them out from before thee, and that he may perform the word which the LORD sware unto thy fathers, Abraham, Isaac, and Jacob. Understand therefore, that the LORD thy God giveth thee not this good land to

> possess it for thy righteousness; for thou art a stiffnecked people. [Deuteronomy 9:5–6]

I had always had trouble with the punishing God of the Old Testament. He is certainly not the loving God I have come to know. Most people feel the same way and prefer to avoid the Old Testament altogether. However, if you read it sequentially and as history, you will come to understand what I came to understand in preparing and writing this book. In reality, it was not God who was evil but the people on Earth who had become so evil.

After seeing what it took for God to get the Israelites on a straight path, I could see why God did not try to straighten out all of humankind at the same time. I could also now understand why God allowed and even aided the Israelites in the destruction of entire cities and the annihilation of its inhabitants. I could better comprehend that God's earlier efforts to destroy everything and start again was not going to lead to success. It had to be a gradual purification process.

The Ark of the Testimony, which began to be called the Ark of the Covenant because of the covenant that God had made with the Israelites, continued to be carried by the Israelites and guarded by the top priests. After Joshua's death and the death of that generation, the Israelites now in the Promised Land somehow forget the covenant and all the things that God had done for their ancestors. As incredible as it may sound, they deserted God and began to worship Baal and other gods. Once again the Israelites disobeyed God.

After Joshua, the Israelites appointed judges to rule them, but they continued to stray from the path of God. Because of this, their conquest of the Promised Land was slow and ineffective. Eventually, the Israelites attributed their misfortunes to the fact that their nation did not have any king to rule them, like other nations in their surroundings. Samuel, the last of the judges, then anointed Saul as the first king of the Israelites.

Had the Israelites *obeyed* God throughout these times, their conquest of the Promised Land would have been easier. God was not happy that the Israelites preferred to be ruled by a king instead of being ruled by Him. But because of free will, He still gave them a chance and supported the newly appointed kings, as long as they showed their *obedience* to Him.

First Saul was anointed, who ruled the Israelites around 1030 to 1010 BC; then followed David, who ruled between 1010 and 970 BC. This is the same David who defeated Goliath when he was a boy. David was a great warrior king and was able to unite the tribes of Israel. He took Jerusalem from the Jebusites around 1000 BC, making it the capital of the Israelites, and he brought the Ark to Jerusalem.

David was followed by the great and wise king Solomon. When Solomon was anointed king, he prayed to God that he might govern according to God's will. God, highly satisfied that Solomon was not asking for anything for himself, rewarded him abundantly with the gift of wisdom. This gift of wisdom allowed Solomon to become the most powerful and rich of all the kings of Israel, admired by neighboring kings and queens.

It is of particular significance that Solomon, in offering his *obedience* to God's will, was so amply rewarded and received so many blessings. He reigned in peace; he and his kingdom became extremely rich and powerful, the envy of neighboring kingdoms. The abundance of God's gifts and blessings has no limit, when we follow Him. We should all consider praying to have the wisdom to discern God's will.

Between 967 and 925 BC, Solomon built the first Jerusalem Temple. It was a magnificent and luxurious Temple, filled with gold decorations and artifacts, and the Ark was installed there, along with all its sacred objects. King Solomon governed very wisely for a long time, but at some point, imbued by power, ego, and his insatiable desire for women (he had some seven hundred wives), he lost the north and started worshiping other gods. He fell into the trap of marrying outside his Israelite faith and giving in to his wives' religious practices. This was the doom of united Israel.

At the end of King Solomon's reign, the Israelites, having again lost direction, fell into disarray. They split this time into Judah and

Israel. Then the Egyptians invaded Jerusalem in 914 BC. Later, Israel was invaded by the Assyrians between 722 and 721 BC. Its inhabitants were deported, and the ten northern tribes of Israel were lost. This left only the tribes of Judah and Benjamin. It was a period of much suffering for the Israelites.

During this time, some of the prophets began announcing the coming of Mary. Mankind had made some progress after all. Toward the latter part of this period, smaller groups of people were attaining high levels of spirituality unknown in the past, leading to the establishment of the Essene community. These people decided to isolate themselves from what was happening in the rest of Israel and Judah. Through the patriarchs, the prophets, and the Israelites of good heart, not everything of the works of God had been lost.

> Therefore the Lord himself shall give you a sign; Behold, a virgin shall conceive, and bear a son, and shall call his name Immanuel. [Isaiah 7:14]

King David was the son of a man called Jesse, and Mary was a direct descendant of David. This quote from the prophet Isaiah (740 BC) makes direct reference to the genealogical tree of Mary and Jesus.

> And there shall come forth a rod out of the stem of Jesse, and a Branch shall grow out of his roots: And the spirit of the LORD shall rest upon him, the spirit of wisdom and understanding, the spirit of counsel and might, the spirit of knowledge and of the fear of the LORD; [Isaiah 11:1–2]

Jeremiah, like Isaiah, also prophesized the coming of Mary:

> Come home, Virgin of Israel, come home to these towns of yours. [Jeremiah 31:22 NJB]

Jeremiah was the prophet around 622 BC, when the last reference to the Ark is found in the Bible. At this time, the Ark with its Blessing was still in the Jerusalem Temple. To protect it from the upcoming Babylonian invasion, it was taken away by Jeremiah and hidden.

> The same document also describes how the prophet, warned by an oracle, gave orders for the tent and the ark to go with him, when he set out for the mountain which Moses had climbed to survey God's heritage. On his arrival, Jeremiah found a cave-dwelling, into which he put the ark and the altar of incense, afterwards blocking up the entrance. [2 Maccabees 2:4–5 NJB]

In 597 BC the Babylonians invaded Jerusalem, and the Temple was plundered and its treasures taken to Babylon. The Ark, however, was not in the Temple any longer. The Ark was to remain lost and forgotten. We only hear about it again when Mary is made aware that She will bear the Son of God. At that time, Mary became the new Ark of the Covenant, since She carried in her womb the Word.

Anne Catherine Emmerich, in her visions, saw similar things happen. She narrates that when the Ark had previously fallen into the hands of the enemy, the Blessing had been removed by the high priests.[2] Before the Babylonian invasion, many centuries earlier in the time of Samuel, the Ark had already been captured by the Philistines, only to be returned because of all the disasters it caused to the captors. [1 Samuel 5:1]

She tells that when Jeremiah hid the Ark along with other precious objects in Mount Sinai, the Blessing was not in it anymore. The Blessing was preserved by the prophet Malachi, and through him it was passed into the hands of the Essenians on Mount Sinai.[3]

After the sacking of the Temple of Jerusalem by the Babylonians and the subsequent destruction and reconstructions that followed, the Temple was again rebuilt at the time of the roman king Herod the

2 *The Lowly*, I, page 114

3 *The Lowly*, I, page 116

Great (74–4 BC), King of Judea. It was in this reconstructed Temple that a second, restored Ark of the Covenant was placed. And it was in this second Ark that the Blessing was placed by an Essenian priest.

> "The place is to remain unknown," he [Jeremiah] said, "until God gathers his people together again and shows them his mercy." [2 Maccabees 2:7 NJB]

Despite many archeological efforts, the original Ark of the Covenant, built by Moses and hidden by Jeremiah, has not yet been discovered, which is a testimony to Jeremiah's prediction. It seems that it is to remain hidden until the time that God decides to "gather His people." I believe that once Mary became the New Ark of the Covenant, the old Ark no longer had any purpose.

The mystery of the Ark of the Covenant had been resolved for me. It not only was a heavy chest that contained the tablets of the law and relics of the patriarchs, but, more importantly, in it was the Blessing that would bring Mary and future salvation to mankind. Although the Israelites did not know what they were protecting in the Ark, they knew it had some spiritual value and protected it for centuries.

Chapter 4

The Essenes and Mary

Before the Babylonian invasion in 597 BC, the prophet Jeremiah hid the Ark of the Covenant and some of its precious objects on Mount Sinai to protect it, and until this day it has never been found. However, the Blessing was removed from the Ark and passed on to the prophet Malachi and then passed on to the Essenes. In this chapter we will try to track down its whereabouts and how it became linked with Mary.

The Essenes were several separate but related Jewish religious groups that shared similar mystic and messianic beliefs, which flourished from the second century BC to the first century AD. The Essenes gained fame in modern times due to the discovery in 1947 of the extensive religious library they maintained for their studies at Qumran known as the Dead Sea Scrolls. The Essenes disappeared towards the end of the first century AD as a result of destructive Roman military campaigns. It seems that they decided to bury the scrolls when they knew destruction was coming their way.

They preserved multiple copies of the Old Testament of the Holy Bible from as early as 300 BC. The multiple copies of the Old Testament in the original Hebrew confirmed the accuracy of the Bible as handed down independently over two thousand years; there were slight changes in wording but not meaning. The Essenes' library also included many other diverse religious texts, providing significant historical insights into various social and religious movements and events around the region.

The other key historical sources of information about the life and beliefs of the Essenes come from the first century Jewish historiographer Flavius Josephus and from Philo, a Jewish philosopher who lived between 20 BC and 50 AD. Josephus' works, entitled *The Jewish War*, written around 73 to 75 AD, and *Antiquities of the Jews*, finished some twenty years later, claim first-hand knowledge of the Essenes. He lists the Essenes as one of the three main sects in "Jewish Philosophy," alongside the Pharisees and the Sadducees. [1]

According to Josephus, Mount Carmel had been the stronghold of the Essenes, who came from a place in Galilee named Nazareth and consequently were sometimes referred to as Nazarenes.[2] We also know from Mary's and Jesus' life that they both lived in Nazareth and that Jesus was also called the Nazarene. Mount Carmel, the sacred mountain in Canaan, can be seen from Nazareth. The renowned prophet Elijah in the ninth century BC also spent time on Mount Carmel.

The Essenes were characterized by their great devotion to God and their frugal lifestyle. They were highly criticized by the two other groups of Israelites, the Pharisees and the Sadducees, because of what they considered the Essenes' extreme life style practices. According to the Dead Sea Scrolls, the Essenes' community school was called "Yahad," meaning "Oneness of God," in order to differentiate themselves from the rest of the Jews, who are repeatedly labeled "The Breakers of the Covenant."[3]

The accounts by Josephus show that some Essenes led a strictly celibate but communal life, while others did get married. This of course

---

1 Essenes. In Wikipedia. Retrieved April 15, 2008, from http://en.wikipedia.org/wiki/Essenes

2 Ibid.

3 Ibid.

had to be the case; otherwise, the Essenes would not have survived as a group. According to Josephus, their customs and observances included collective ownership, electing and following a leader; they were forbidden from swearing oaths and sacrificing animals.[4]

They controlled their tempers and served as channels of peace, carried weapons only as protection against robbers, had no slaves and instead served each other, and, as a result of communal ownership, did not engage in trading. They were committed to practicing piety towards God and righteousness towards humanity, to maintaining a pure lifestyle, to abstaining from criminal and immoral activities, to transmitting their rules uncorrupted, and to preserving the books of the Essenes. Their theology included belief in the immortality of the soul and that they would receive their souls back after death.[5]

In 1947, when the famous Dead Sea scrolls came to light, a wealth of potential new information about the Essenes was revealed, which even now has not been fully transcribed nor fully understood. Numerous old texts confirming biblical books of the Old Testament, as well as several other works that do not match biblical books of the New Testament and are called the Apocrypha Gospels, have been translated. There is much debate going on right now as to the veracity of the Apocrypha Gospels, but it is not relevant here to delve into this debate.

Anne Catherine Emmerich also makes substantial references to the Essenes, even though not much was known of them in her time (1774 to 1824), before the Dead Sea Scrolls were discovered, which further confirms the accuracy of her visions. She corroborates much of what Josephus and Philo recorded and also mentions the Essenian ability to heal using their hands.

Mount Carmel is also the place where many of Elijah's followers were established to venerate God and prepare for the coming of Mary. Carmelite tradition suggests that a community of Jewish hermits had lived at the site from the time of Elijah until the Carmelites were

4 Ibid.

5 Ibid.

founded there. The Carmelite Constitution of 1281 claims that from the time when Elijah dwelt on Mount Carmel, priests and prophets, Jewish and Christian, had lived praiseworthy lives in holy penitence during an uninterrupted succession. It is very likely then that the Essenes are the successors of Elijah.

The healing abilities of the Essenes could also have their origins in the healing abilities of Elijah and his successor, Elisha. Aside from Jesus, there are only two other quotes in the Old Testament that I could find of people being brought back to life. The first one corresponds to Elijah [1 Kings 17:21–22] and the second one corresponds to Elisha. [2 Kings 4:32–35] In both cases, a boy is brought back to life; the way in which the prophets do this is by using their own bodies to heal the individual. Christ, later on, performed many miraculous healings by laying His hands on the sick, and the practice of laying hands continues to this day.

In my own experience, humans have the capability to heal others by the use of their hands, and there are many techniques used in our times for this. I have studied only two: Reiki and LaHoChi. It all started several years ago, after I watched Beatriz, my wife, heal people using her hands. Through the laying of her hands and by becoming a conduit, Beatriz was allowing God to do the healing work through her. I decided I had to put my limiting paradigms aside and open myself to these kinds of things.

We know from Anne Catherine Emmerich's visions that Mary's ancestors were closely related to the Essenes. Her grandfather was an Essene. The high priests of the Essenes, who resided on Mount Sinai, also called Mount Horeb, were frequently consulted by Mary's female ancestors to determine whom they should marry to preserve the lineage and make possible the coming of Mary. Elijah had also resided on Mount Sinai, and there is a well-known cave that is believed to be associated with him, which was used by the high Essene priests.

Anne Catherine Emmerich makes several references to the contents of the Ark of the Covenant and its relationship with Mary's ancestors. In one of these, she narrates how Anna's grandmother (Mary's great-grandmother), was receiving counsel from the high priest of the Essenes at the time (Archos), and she clearly describes contents of the Ark of the Covenant being in the hands of the high Essenes priest. The narration is long, so I will summarize it the best I can.[6]

Anna's grandmother, Emorun, went to the high priest Archos on Horeb for him to decide from among several suitors whom she was to accept in marriage. Archos, as the Levite priests did when they approached the Ark, put on his ceremonial vestments for prophesying. He ascended the many steps to the top of Mount Horeb (Mount Sinai) and entered the cave of Elijah, where the relics that contained the Blessing were kept. This Blessing was the one that for centuries had been in the Ark of the Covenant, which contained the secret of the coming of the Blessed Virgin. There he placed himself in prayer, seeking an answer.

In the cave vaulting was a hole through which light filtered, illuminating the interior. Against the wall was a little altar carved out of the rock, upon which rested several sacred objects. On the altar, in the middle between some little bushes of herbs, was a little tree, with leaves that looked yellowish and were twisted like snail shells, making Anne Catherine think of the tree of Jesse, from Isaiah's prophecy.

On this little tree, the high priest Archos could predict how soon the coming of the Blessed Virgin was to be expected. It looked as if the tree had grown out of Aaron's rod, which had once been in the Ark of the Covenant. When Mary's ancestors came to Archos for marriage guidance, like this, Archos took the rod of Aaron into his hand and prayed in the same way for a revelation. If the marriage was destined to take its place in Mary's ancestry line, the rod put forth a bud, which produced one or more flowers. The high priest would then interpret this and select the suitor.

When Archos finished his prayers and came out of the cave, he went and announced to Emorun the prophetic knowledge that had been revealed to him. He told her that she should marry her sixth

---

6 *The Lowly*, I, 120–129

suitor and that she would bear a child marked with a sign, who was chosen as a vessel in preparation for the coming of the Savior.

So Emorun married her sixth suitor, an Essene called Stolanus, and had three daughters: Ismeria, Emerintia, and Enue. Emerintia married Aphras, or Ophras, a Levite, and of this marriage was born Elisabeth, the mother of John the Baptist. Ismeria married Eliud. They lived after the manner of the married Essenes in the region of Nazareth; Anna, the mother of Mary, was one of their children.

Anna's father, Eliud, was of the tribe of Levi; her mother, Ismeria, was of the tribe of Benjamin. Anna was born at Bethlehem, but afterwards her parents moved to Sephoris, four hours from Nazareth, where they had a house and land. They also owned land in the beautiful valley of Zabulon, three hours from Nazareth.

Anne's parents were very pious, devout, charitable, simple, and upright. They often divided their possessions into three equal parts and gave one third to the Temple. The other third they gave to the poor, in accordance with Essene principles. The third part they kept for themselves. Because of this charitable approach to life, the third part they kept quickly multiplied and increased in abundance, so that they were able to divide it into three again.

In her fifth year, Anna was taken to the school in the Temple, where she remained twelve years. She was brought home again in her seventeenth year. A year after this, Ismeria fell mortally ill. As she lay dying, she spoke alone with Anna, telling her that she was the chosen vessel of grace and that she must marry following the counsel of the prophet at Mount Horeb.

Anna's father was often with his family in the valley of Zabulon, and after Ismeria's death he moved there altogether. This led to the connection with the parents of Joachim, Anna's future husband. Anna had at least six suitors, but she rejected them all. After taking counsel, like her ancestors, with the Essene high priest, she was directed to marry Joachim. He was a pious, holy man and was poor, whereas Anna came from a rich family. Anna was about nineteen years old when she married Joachim.

Anna and Joachim's first-born was a daughter, Maria Heli, but since at her birth she did not exhibit the signs that had been predicted, they concluded she was not the child of promise. For nineteen years after the birth of Maria Heli, they lived their lives dedicated to God, in constant yearning, praying for the blessing of the promised child, but Anna remained barren. Anna and Joachim lived in a house near Nazareth. Here they would divide their possessions in three parts, as Anne's parents had: one third for the Temple, one third for the Essenes, and one third for themselves.

The Importance of Charity

Charity is so important in life because it helps us walk down the path of *non-judgment*. You well know that God asks us not to judge others, but what happens in our minds most of the day when we see and talk to other people? We are constantly judging them. What happens when we see a beggar in the street? Don't we go straight to our worse judging behavior? We justify ourselves in not contributing money to this person on the basis of these judgments. "I will not fund this person's alcoholic behavior," we say to ourselves, without even knowing if the person drinks alcohol.

When you give to someone without asking questions, without judging—because only God knows the circumstances of this person—without expecting anything in return, you are expressing the most pure love that God the father created in the universe. It puts in motion an incredible mechanism, a very sophisticated mechanism that only God was able to conceive, where one thing leads to another, and this thing leads to another, and another, and another, until it returns to you in a marvelous way, often multiplied for your benefit. It comes from the strangest places, always unexpected but nevertheless delightful.

Many years ago, my very good friend Luis Castro, a university philosophy teacher and coach of our rugby team, was struggling with his health. He was renting a small basement apartment while he finished remodeling a house he had purchased. This apartment was very humid, and he was experiencing a lot of respiratory problems. He had run out of money to finish his house; the longer he waited, the more his dream of completing the house drifted away. The house was deteriorating rapidly; people were stealing fixtures and materials from the house.

I told him I would help him finish his house and that he did not have to worry about paying me until he could. It was a complicated time in my life because I had just quit my job at the multinational company after thirteen years and was starting my own business. So I did not have a steady income anymore. Despite this, I felt it was right to help him out, because Luis had done so much for me and was always there to help others. He had been like my second father, guiding me and helping me make the most of the gifts God gave me. Luis, like most people would, refused my offer and did not want me to do the work. He was not sure he was going to be able to pay me back.

In the end, I managed to convince him, and we started the work. After several months and several tens of thousands of dollars, the house was finished and he could move in. This was a very happy moment for all of us. Luis hosted an open house party for all his friends, specially the rugby team friends who were very close to him. I never gave Luis a statement and never told him how much he owed me. Whenever he asked me, I would say, "Don't worry, we will deal with this later."

Not long after the house had been finished, I received a call from my former employer, telling me I had a check there that I needed to pick up. They explained that my termination payment had been miscalculated and that they had underpaid me. 'Well', I thought, 'that is great; some additional cash will be very welcome now, when I have no salary,' so I rushed to pick up the check, thinking that maybe it was a few thousand dollars. To my complete surprise, the amount of the check was huge. It was exactly the amount of money I had put toward finishing Luis' house. When I say exactly, I mean exactly.

This was not a coincidence, nor was it a miracle; it was just the mechanism of charity at work. Whatever you give to charity or people in need returns back to you, often many times over. In this case, since it was a large sum of money, the message from God could not be clearer. Isn't it incredible? It is like the practice of Mary's ancestors, who gave away one third of their wealth to the poor and had it return to them, multiplied.

I now always give without asking questions. I know that my reward for giving money to that beggar in the street is in Heaven. I give and do not judge. I am now, by the grace of God, able to love the beggar, instead of criticizing him. We do not know the story of the man, what led him to this place. How can we then judge him fairly? *Charity is one of the ways in which we manifest the virtue of nonjudgment.*

When we give, we should not brag about it but instead keep it between God and ourselves. That is how we receive God's grace. I had trouble sharing this story with you; not even Beatriz knew about it. But I think that in the context of this book and because it really drives the point home, it was worth making an exception.

Time magazine named Bill and Melinda Gates and rock star Bono as its "Persons of the Year" in 2005, citing their charitable work and activism aimed at reducing global poverty and improving world health. I saved the article because I was impressed with their efforts. In that year Bill Gates was the richest man in the world, with about $47 billion dollars of net worth. He was also the world's biggest philanthropist, giving $27 billion dollars to the Bill and Melinda Gates Foundation.

The foundation ended 2007 with $38.7 billion dollars available for charitable activities. It is simply staggering the amount of money that Bill Gates has donated to charitable purposes. In 2007 he donated another $1.3 billion in cash. His good friend Warren Buffet, who joined ranks with Bill Gates' foundation a few years back, donated $1.8 billion in Berkshire-Hathaway stock in 2007.

Bono in 2005 "charmed and bullied and morally blackmailed the leaders of the world's richest countries into forgiving $40 billion in dept owed by the poorest," the magazine said. Senator Jesse Helms praised him in the following words: "I knew as soon as I met Bono that he was genuine." These people are doing so much good with their wealth and their talents and at the same time can remain so humble, that you have to be impressed by their example. Giving your time and your talents is service, which is another form of charity.

Continuing with Anne Catherine Emmerich's visions, Joachim took the corresponding offerings to the Temple in Jerusalem, but he was not kindly welcomed by one of the priests. The gifts were disdained because of Joachim's and Anna's inability to produce the promised child, and Joachim was reproached publicly. He was so grieved and ashamed at having been rejected in the Temple that he left home and remained in hiding for five months.[7]

Anna learned of Joachim's humiliation in the Temple through others and also suffered greatly. She spent long hours in prayer and penitence, until finally one day an angel of God appeared to her on the patio of her house and told her she was to go to the Temple the next day to meet Joachim under the Golden Gate; her husband had received a like message. Anna was filled with joy; her prayers and intentions had finally been answered. When she fell asleep that night, the angel of God appeared to her again.

> When after her lengthy prayer, she lay on her couch asleep I saw light descending upon her. It surrounded her, yes, even penetrated her. I saw her, upon an interior perception, tremblingly awake and sit upright. Near her, to the right, she saw a luminous figure writing on the wall in large, shinning Hebrew characters. I read and understood the writing word for word. It was to this effect that she should conceive, that the fruit of her womb should be altogether special, and that the Blessing received by Abraham was to be the source of this conception. [*The Lowly*, I, 133]

When Anna woke up after midnight, she realized that the name MARY had been written in the wall in large, shining golden-red letters. Anna was at the time forty-three years old.

Joachim was going through difficult times. It had been five months since he had gone away. With great perseverance, he tended his flock

---

7 *The Lowly*, I, 130-133

of lambs on Mount Hermon beyond the Jordan, constantly praying to God to grant him his supplications. Remember that it had been nineteen years since Maria Heli, their first daughter, had been born. During all this time, both Joachim and Anna prayed fervently for another child; the child of promise.

Intention Prayer

We all have intentions that we pray for fervently, like Anna and Joachim did. Sometimes our prayers are answered, and other times they are not. What makes an intention prayer more likely to be answered? I believe that when our intentions are aligned with God's will for our lives, they are more easily answered. When we elevate these prayers through Mary, all the better.

> Mary's Message of July 25, 2008, from Medjugorje: "Dear children! At this time when you are thinking of physical rest, I call you to conversion. Pray and work so that your heart yearns for God the Creator who is the true rest of your soul and your body. May He reveal His face to you and may He give you His peace. I am with you and *intercede before God for each of you.* Thank you for having responded to my call." [www.medjugorje.org]

I have realized in my own life that miracles do happen and that, at least to some extent, through our own free will, we can make these miracles happen for us. Let me explain. About five years ago, I wrote on a white piece of paper what I wanted my life to be in five years. There is something magical about taking your thoughts and putting them on paper. We think we know what we want when we are just in the thought stage, but when we have to write the thoughts down, we realize that we really do not know. When we write them down and realize that these thoughts can become a reality, we begin to have doubts. We ask ourselves: Is this really what I want?

Writing your thoughts down will take some time the first time around. You will have to do many edits until you get it to a comfortable stage. Once you finish, you must set the paper aside and wait a couple of days. Then return and read it again. If you are still satisfied with what you wrote, then this will become your "My Intentions" prayer. If you are not happy, just make the necessary changes and meditate over it for a few more days until you get it right.

This exercise is necessary for the miracles you wish for your life. God gave us free will, and He will be happy to deliver the life we want as long as it is inspired in God's goodness. God wants us to be happy, to be peaceful, and to no longer experience soul sufferings. He wants us to return to Paradise as the enlightened beings we can be, in His likeness. However, we will not accomplish this if our intention prayers are filled with material things, with pursuit of power and ego building. If your intentions are full of such things, God cannot help, and you will have to do the entire job.

Let me share the example of My Intentions prayer from five years ago, with the hope of shedding some light on this. In the first paragraph, it says:

> "It is my intention to devote each day of my life to bring peace and love to the world and to bring forward the Christ essence."

Notice how broad and God-inspired this first intention is. I did not write down, "I want to write a book," although I had wanted to write one for a long time. I did not write that I wanted to have a million dollars or be the CEO of a corporation. This does not mean that God does not want material wealth for us, or that He does not want power for us. You can have either or both, as long as they are God-inspired and not ego-inspired. These things will come to your life as a consequence of first achieving the spiritual goals that God desires for your life. You will notice that the second intention in my prayer does include a strong reference to wealth:

> "I am doing this alongside my loving spouse, Beatriz, in abundant health and in abundant economic wealth."

When I compare My Intention prayer of five years ago with my life today, it is exactly the same. God delivered everything on my Intentions list. Broader statements are better. I am doing my part to bring peace and love to the world and, through my example, to bring forward the Christ essence. In writing this book, I firmly believe I will be able to touch many more people. Mary through Her maternal love can effectively bring many of Her children back home, like She did with me.

I wrote that I wanted to live in a place where I could be in communion with nature, where I would not be bogged down by traffic and where I could find time for creativity and meditation and time for pleasure.

> "We live in beautiful, peaceful places that allow our inspiration and creativity to reach its maximum potential and where our children have the proper environment for their development into better human beings. I have time to share many wonderful moments with my spouse, our children and loved ones, and time to play, laugh, and enjoy the beauty of the world.
>
> Our house is gorgeous and very comfortable for our family's size and is close to work, schools, and friends. It is a safe place, always protected by the mighty beings of light of the highest. There is much space to play and to contemplate, meditate, and heal, surrounded by beautiful natural elements."

I have a beautiful, loving wife and the best five children I could have hoped for. They all are very responsible and doing well in their respective studies. Arianna will graduate in 2009 with a major in engineering and a minor in anthropology from Carnegie Mellon University. Andres is a freshman at Cornell University, where he is studying architecture. Alex is graduating this year from high school and is working hard to get accepted in a good university. Andrea is excelling as a freshman in high school, and Sofia, the youngest, is also excelling in middle school. Five out of five is not a bad record! I am so proud of my children; I could not ask for more.

Notice I did not place limits or fix specific places. I did not ask for more than my family and I needed. The more open you are with your intentions, the easier it is for God to move the strings of the Universe and deliver your intentions. In another paragraph, I wrote:

> "I am open to Divine guidance so I may be more effective at accomplishing my mission. I write, teach, heal, and lead using my talents, which are many, thank God, and through this Divine guidance my efforts yield extraordinary results."

When you tell God that you are open to "Divine Guidance," He can lead you along the way, and God rejoices so much. If you leave Him space in your intentions to maneuver, that's better. It is not that you are relinquishing your free will or that you are losing purpose in your life. It is and becomes exactly the opposite. You are applying yourself, all your talents and your will, to pursue a higher cause that will be aided by God and thus easier to attain. I close My Intentions prayer with the following statement:

> "As I help other human beings move toward Nova beings and help anchor Nova Earth, I am the perfect manifestation of an enlightened being."

Nova beings signify, for me, our awakened state of communion with God. Nova Earth is of course Earth, inhabited by Nova beings, regaining the beautiful essence and balance that we were originally endowed with. When I wrote this several years ago, I did not have the level of understanding that I have today; not that I believe I have reached enlightenment. I wish that were true in my case. But I am awakening a little every day, with the help of Mary, who brings me closer to God every day.

The power of writing down your intentions cannot be underestimated. How else does God, or the universe if you prefer, know what you really want? Before I wrote My Intentions, I was sending confusing signals to the universe. One day I wanted this, another day I wanted that. This was because my intentions were very specific, as opposed to being broad in nature, as they ended up in the written version. If your intentions are aligned with God's intentions, you will see them manifest very quickly. Five years is not a long time for such profound changes as the ones I have achieved in my life.

Most importantly, the end result is not going to be anything you anticipated. It will be better! I never thought in my wildest dreams that I would be living in Arizona. My radar was aimed towards North Carolina and its vicinity. Here I am today, living in Sedona, named one of the very best U.S. travel destination by newspapers and travel organizations. I never thought I would become a successful writer and work so close to home that I do not actually have to leave my house. This place is so safe that we don't lock our house or our cars. Everything is close: schools, supermarket, cinemas, etc. God has delivered beyond my expectations!

The aspect of My Intentions that I am still struggling with is how I can become "the perfect manifestation of an enlightened being." I believe I know the answer, at least in theory, and it is expressed through this book. But I have a long way to go to achieve a consistent practice of the same things that I am describing here. My struggles are the same as yours. I may be a little further ahead of some along the path and, at the same time, way behind others in this quest for enlightenment.

I know, for instance, that charity and service are big components, and I am not doing nearly enough. I know that being silent in contemplative prayer, in the stillness of meditation for considerable time, is also a requirement, but I am still "doing" too many things throughout the day, instead of "being." You have heard the expression, "We are human doings, instead of human beings." Try writing your own spiritually inspired "My Intentions" prayer now, and you will see how God responds.

After nineteen years, Anna and Joachim had their prayers answered. It was a huge request, but it was also one that was aligned with Divine Guidance. Anna knew she had an important role in bringing the Messiah. Her mother had told her this, although she did not know when He was to come, much less that she was going to be His grandmother. One day, the angel of God appeared to Joachim as he had to Anna:

> The angel commanded him to take his offering up to the Temple, promised that his prayer should be heard, and told him that he should pass under the Golden Gate. At this announcement, Joachim was troubled. He felt very timid about going again to the Temple. But the angel assured him that the priests had already been enlightened with regard to him." [*The Lowly*, I, 134]

> ... and I saw two priests go out to Joachim and lead him through the side-apartments into the Sanctuary before the altar of incense... The priests immediately retired to a distance and left Joachim alone before the altar. I saw him on his knees, his arms extended, while the incense offering slowly consumed itself. He remained shut up in the Temple all night, praying with great and ardent desires. I saw that he was in ecstasy. A luminous figure appeared to him in the same manner as to Zachary, and gave him a roll written in shining letters. On it were the three names: Helia, Hanna, Mirjam[8], and near the last one the picture of a little Ark of the Covenant, or tabernacle. Joachim laid the roll on his breast under his garment. The angel spoke: "Anne will conceive an immaculate child from whom the Redeemer of the world will be born." The angel told him moreover not to grieve over his sterility which was not a disgrace to him, but a glory, for that what his spouse would conceive should not be from him, a fruit from God, the culmination point of the Blessing given to Abraham. Then the angel led him behind the curtain that concealed the grating before the Holy of Holies. [*The Lowly*, I, 135]
>
> The angel now removed something from the Ark of the Covenant, though without opening the door. It was the Mystery of the Ark, the Sacrament of the Incarnation, the Immaculate

8 These names are other forms of Joachim, Anna, and Mary

> Conception, the Consummation of the Blessing of Abraham. I beheld it under the appearance of a luminous body. The angel blessed or anointed Joachim's forehead with the tip of his thumb and forefinger; then he slipped the shining body under Joachim's garment and it entered into him, how I can not say. He also gave him something to drink out of a glittering chalice which he held supported by two fingers. The chalice was of the same shape as that used at the Last Supper, but without a foot. Joachim was directed to take it with him and keep it at his home. [*The Lowly*, I, 136]

Then the angel left, and Joachim was left in ecstasy, almost paralyzed. The priests then came back to the Holy of Holies and found him in this state. They helped him up and had him sit in a place reserved for the priests. Once Joachim had recovered from his almost unconscious state, he was filled with much joy and looked young and radiant. He was once again guided from above to go to the Golden Gate, where he was to meet with Anna. The priests led him to a tunnel, or subterranean passage, which belonged to the consecrated part of the Temple and ran beneath it, which would take him to the Golden Gate.

Anna had also come to the Temple at that time. After delivering her offerings, she had confessed to a priest that an angel of God had come to her and that she was to meet her husband under the Golden Gate of the Temple. Anna was led by the priest to the other side of the passage that Joachim had entered. They both walked and met in a place where there was a pillar in the form of a palm tree with hanging fruits and leaves. And it was here, under the Golden Gate of the Temple, that Mary's Immaculate Conception took place.[9]

After this long period of struggles and purification of the human race, finally the Blessing had found a home in the Essene community; a group of people that had surrendered to God; they had achieved a level of purity and holiness not known until that time. And amongst the Essenes there finally was a human worth carrying the seed of the

9 *The Lowly*, I, 138

incarnate Mary, God's Second Eternal Thought. The whole of God's creation rejoiced in this long awaited event that would bring the hope of mankind's salvation to life.

Chapter 5

Immaculate Conception and Purity of Body

The Immaculate Conception refers to the creation of a new human being in the womb of the mother, without sexual intercourse by the parents. This new human being is conceived solely from spirit, the Holy Spirit, and is created in all purity, "full of grace," therefore free from original sin. The rest of us mortals carry within our blueprints the Fall from God's grace of our first parents, Adam and Eve, which naturally predisposes us towards the bondage of sin. It's worth noting that disobedience is the sin; not sex, which is good because it was created by God.

Many people, including me in the past, are confused by the concept of the "Immaculate Conception." Most people believe that Immaculate Conception refers to the conception of Jesus in Mary's womb in an immaculate way. However, after reading Anne Catherine Emmerich, I really understood that the Immaculate Conception of Mary refers to "Her" Immaculate Conception and not that of Her son Jesus.

Wow! How could it be that after more than five years of actively participating in my faith, I finally find this out? I started asking relatives and friends what they understood about the Immaculate Conception, and most of the answers, generally nine out of ten, had the wrong response, associating it with Jesus and not Mary. Why was this information not more widely known? For me, this was another incredible finding, another key piece of the puzzle.

Then I looked into the Catholic Church's doctrine to understand the Church's point of view regarding Mary's Immaculate Conception. What I found puzzled me even more. The Roman Catholic Church itself did not acknowledge Mary's Immaculate Conception until the fifteenth century. Why was that, if there had been a strong popular belief in this much earlier? Since the creation of the Christian church, Church Fathers wrote about and believed in the Immaculate Conception.

It wasn't until 1476 that Pope Sixtus IV established the feast for Mary's Immaculate Conception on December 8. He did not define the doctrine as a dogma, thus leaving Roman Catholics free to believe in it or not[1].

This freedom to believe in the Immaculate Conception was reiterated by the Council of Trent, held between 1545 and 1563. The Council of Trent was the nineteenth Ecumenical Council of the Roman Catholic Church, considered one of the Church's most important councils. Ecumenical means that it was open to all the Church, including dissenting factions of the Church associated with the Protestant Reformation.[2]

---

1 Immaculate conception. In Wikipedia, the free encyclopedia. Retrieved May 5, 2008, from http://en.wikipedia.org/wiki/Immaculate_conception.

2 The Protestant Reformation was a reform movement that began in 1517, though its roots lie further back in time. The Reformation involved cultural, economic, political, and religious aspects. It began with Martin Luther and ended in 1648. The movement began as an attempt to reform the Catholic Church. Many western Catholics were troubled by what they saw as false doctrines and malpractices within the Church, particularly involving the teaching and sale of indulgences. Another major contention was the practice of buying and selling church positions (simony) and what was seen as systemic, even reaching the position of the Pope. On October 31, 1517, in Saxony (in what is now Germany), Martin Luther nailed his Ninety-Five Theses to the door of the Wittenberg Castle Church, which served as a notice board for university-related announcements. These were points for debate that criticized the Church and the Pope. The most controversial points centered on the practice of selling indulgences and the Church's policy on Purgatory. Other beliefs and practices under attack by Protestant reformers included devotion to Mary, or Mariology, the intercession of and devotion to the saints, most of the sacraments, mandatory celibacy requirement of its clergy and the authority of the Pope. The most important denominations to emerge directly from

In 1534, Henry VIII had already turned his back on the Pope and become Supreme Head of the Church of England, giving rise to Anglicanism. Protestantism, Lutheranism, and Calvinism threatened to do the same if the Church did not make the required reforms. The Council of Trent's ratification of the freedom to believe in the Immaculate Conception during these troubled times indicated where the minds of most of the Church's representatives stood with regards to the Immaculate Conception.

Finally on December 8, 1854, the Immaculate Conception was defined as a dogma by Pope Pius IX. The Roman Catholic Church believes the dogma is supported by Scripture: Mary's being greeted by Angel Gabriel as "full of grace," or "highly favored," Mary being called the Blessed Virgin in Luke's Gospel. It is also supported by *sensus fidei*, or "sense of the faith," as well as directly or indirectly by the writings of many of the Church Fathers, in the early times of the nascent Christian faith. Catholic theology maintains that, since Jesus became incarnate of the Virgin Mary, it was fitting that she be completely free of sin.[3]

The Immaculate Conception dogma was not supported by the nascent Reformist churches. Pope Pius IX defined this dogma unilaterally, without consultation with the other churches. Neither Eastern Orthodox churches, nor the Anglican Communion, nor the various Protestant communities share the dogma. Orthodox Christians do believe that Mary was without sin for her entire life, but they generally do not share the Roman Catholic Church's views on original sin. Anglo-Catholics also accept the dogma.

---

the Reformation were the Lutherans, the Reformed/Calvinists/Presbyterians, and the Anabaptists. [Protestant Reformation. In Wikipedia, the free encyclopedia. Retrieved May 5, 2008, from http://en.wikipedia.org/wiki/Protestant_reformation

3 While most Catholic doctrines and theological teachings either originate in scripture or are established by the higher levels of the Church hierarchy, sensus fidelium works from the ground up, from the beliefs of the masses of the faithful, as inspired by the Holy Spirit left by Jesus Christ to guide the faithful at large within the framework of the Catholic Church. The catechism of the Catholic Church states that: Christ fulfills this prophetic office, not only by the hierarchy, but also by the laity. He accordingly both establishes them as witnesses and provides them with the sense of the faith [sensus fidei] and the grace of the word. [Sensus fidelium. In Wikipedia, the free encyclopedia. Retrieved May 5, 2008, from http://en.wikipedia.org/wiki/Sensus_fidei]

Because of the divergent positions on this issue by other Christian denominations, the dogma was not promoted more strongly, and the Roman Catholic Church took a rather quiet approach to the Immaculate Conception. This would explain why such an important faith building block was left behind and why it did not permeate in a more broad way to our time.

It took eighteen centuries for Mary's Immaculate Conception to be officially recognized by the Church. But it only took four years for Mary to respond. In 1858 in Lourdes, France, Mary appeared to a fourteen-year-old girl, Bernadette Soubirous, and identified Herself as "The Immaculate Conception." This was very significant at the time because it confirmed the recently established dogma.

Anne Catherine Emmerich's vision of the Immaculate Conception of Mary, when Anna and Joachim met under the Golden Gate in the Temple, is very revealing.

> I saw Joachim and Anne embrace each other in ecstasy. They were surrounded by hosts of angels, some floating over them carrying a luminous tower like that which we see in the pictures of the Litany of Loretto. The tower vanished between Joachim and Anne, both of whom were encompassed by brilliant light and glory. At the same moment the heavens above them opened, and I saw the joy of the Most Holy Trinity and of the angels over the Conception of Mary. Both Joachim and Anne were in a supernatural state. I learned that, at the moment in which they embraced and the light shone around them, the Immaculate Conception of Mary was accomplished. [*The Lowly*, I, 138]

Complete Union with God

Mary was begotten by Anna and Joachim only after they had completely surrendered to God. Perfect surrender to God means conquering our egos. It means getting out of the trap of the mind, which is permanently trying to bring our attention to the physical aspects of our life. My mind does not want me to meditate and shut it off; nor does it want me to focus on God and ignore it. It wants me to keep busy "doing" things of all sorts, instead of just "being." When we can separate thinking from being, we reach complete union with God.

What are the practical things we can do that will help us achieve complete surrender to God, perfect union with God? Mary gives us the answer through Her messages in Medjugorje. She says: seek God through prayer with an open heart.

> Message of Our Lady to Mirjana Soldo on November 2, 2008: "Dear children, today I call you to *a complete union with God.* Your body is on earth, but I ask you for your soul to be all the more often in God's nearness. You will achieve this through *prayer, prayer with an open heart...*" [www.medjugorje.net]

There are many ways to pray, but the most effective one is to pray with an open heart, as Mary says. I pray every day, several times a day, and I try as much as I can to be in a constant state of prayer. My prayer may be the "Our Father" or the "Hail Mary," or just an open conversation. The "Our Father," or "Lord's Prayer," was handed down to us by Jesus. [Matthew 6:9–13 & Luke 11:2–4] The first two sentences of the "Hail Mary" come from two passages of the Gospel of Luke [Luke 1:28 & Luke 1:42] when Archangel Gabriel speaks to Mary, and the last sentence was added at the Council of Trent of 1566. Mary asks us in particular to pray the rosary every day, during which we should also make our intentions for peace in our lives and in the world.

> Mary's Message of January 25, 1991, from Medjugorje: "Dear children! Today, like never before, I invite you to prayer. Let your prayer be a prayer for peace. Satan is strong and desires to destroy not only human life, but also nature and the planet on which you live. Therefore, dear children, pray that through prayer you can protect yourselves with God's blessing of peace. God has sent me among you so that I may help you. If you so wish, grasp for the *rosary*. Even the *rosary* alone can work miracles in the world and in your lives. I

> bless you and I remain with you for as long as it is God's will. Thank you for not betraying my presence here and I thank you because your response is serving the good and the peace." [www.medjugorje.net]

The rosary was given to Saint Dominic of the church of Prouille, France, by Mary in the year 1214. Saint Dominic, because of people's sins, had withdrawn into a forest near Toulouse, where he prayed continuously for three days and three nights. During this time, he did harsh penances, which led him into coma. At this point, Mary appeared to him and said, "Dear Dominic, do you know which weapon the Blessed Trinity wants to use to reform the world?" "Oh, my Lady," answered Saint Dominic, "you know far better than I do, because next to your Son Jesus Christ you have always been the chief instrument of our salvation." Then Mary replied, "I want you to know that, in this kind of warfare, the principal weapon has always been the Angelic Psalter, which is the foundation-stone of the New Testament. Therefore, if you want to reach these hardened souls and win them over to God, preach my Psalter."[4]

At the time of Saint Dominic, the rosary was called the Psalter of Jesus and Mary, because it had the same number of Hail Marys as there are psalms in the Book of the Psalms of David. Since simple and uneducated people were not able to say the Psalms of David, the rosary was prayed in its place. In 1460, Blessed Alan de la Roche, a follower of St. Dominic, reestablished the prayer of the Psalter, which by that time had fallen into disuse, but he started calling it the rosary. Mary appeared to him and said, "You were a great sinner in your youth, but I obtained the grace of your conversion from my Son. Had such a thing been possible, I would have liked to have gone through all kinds of suffering to save you, because converted sinners are a glory to me. And I would have done that also to make you worthy of preaching my rosary far and wide."[5]

Bernadette Soubirous, the seer of Lourdes, stated that in her

---

4 Secret of the Rosary, Saint Louis De Montfort

5 Ibid.

initial meeting with Mary, "The Lady took the rosary that she held in her hands and she made the sign of the cross." The apparitions of Mary in Fatima, Portugal, are sometimes also called Our Lady of the rosary because Mary specifically identified Herself as "the Lady of the Rosary." The three children at Our Lady of Fatima stated they were asked to pray the rosary every day, reiterating many times that the rosary was the key to personal and world peace.

There is a remarkable story of a miracle of the rosary at Hiroshima, where the atomic bomb was dropped on August 6, 1945, destroying the whole town and killing one hundred and forty thousand people. Just a few blocks distant, less than a mile away from the place where the bomb landed, was a home with a small church attached to it. The explosion destroyed the church but left the home intact and, within it, the eight German Jesuit missionaries who lived there.

All eight priests prayed the rosary every day. They miraculously survived the destructive force of the atomic explosion and went on to live normal lives afterwards. Scientists could never find an explanation for the miracle. "We believe that we survived because we were living the message of Fatima," said Fr. Schiffer, one of the survivors. In 1973, also in Japan, Mary appeared to Sister Agnes Sasagawa in Akita and told her, "Pray very much the prayers of the rosary. I alone am able still to save you from the calamities which approach."

When I pray the rosary, it is a meditation for me; a quiet, intimate conversation with Mary. Praying the rosary is like repeating a mantra over and over, as is done and has been done for ages by other religions and spiritual practices. The repetition of a mantra allows us to quiet our minds and our spirits to grow. It is an excellent tool to help us get a step closer to enlightenment. Although the rosary has existed since 1214, prayer beads and strings with cords had been used much earlier than that and are used in many religious faiths today. Please do not allow religious obstacles to get in the way of the beautiful prayer of the rosary. Or if you prefer, pray your own version or mantra.

Beatriz and I now pray the rosary together every night, and we make a special intention for the establishment of peace on Earth.

We know that Mary happily receives our prayers and thanks us for acknowledging Her requests and for taking the time to be with Her. When I am praying the rosary, I feel Mary's presence so clearly that I know She receives my words and acts as my advocate before Jesus. I now have a need, or dependency, for the rosary; I am a proud man of the rosary. To find out more about the rosary, please refer to Appendix I.

Mary also asks for fasting. In Medjugorje, She specifically asks us to fast twice a week, on Wednesdays and Fridays. Fasting is to abstain for twenty-four hours from all food and drink, except necessary water and small amounts of bread to keep our headaches away and our bodies working. I have discovered in fasting that water alone has the unusual effect of taking away hunger. Many times, even when I am not fasting, taking a glass of water will take away that sensation of hunger.

> Mary's Message of October 25, 2008, from Medjugorje: "... little children, arm yourselves with prayer and *fasting* so that you may be conscious of how much God loves you and may carry out God's will..." [www.medjugorje.org]

The purpose of fasting is to remind us throughout the day of the intentions of our prayers and for us to be conscious of God in our lives. This is a very effective practice in this hectic world, where our attention is permanently diverted to outside events, where our ego wants us to live. Fasting helps us separate our physical needs and our ego from our spirit. In attaining this separation and focusing attention on our spirit, we again come a step closer to enlightenment.

Fasting also helps us purify our bodies and earns us graces, an indispensable requirement for enlightenment. Our body is the temple of the Holy Spirit, and as such it needs to be tended and cared for. Remember that Jesus and Mary both have their bodies with them in Heaven. They were able to keep them because their bodies were sufficiently pure.

> Or do you not know that your body is the temple of the Holy Spirit who is in you, whom you have from God, and you are not your own? [1 Corinthians 6:19 NJB]

Although I have made incredible progress in controlling and minimizing my ego through prayer and fasting, I am not yet where Mary wants me to be. She is for me the best example of someone who conquered the ego, of exemplary humbleness, and I am constantly trying to imitate Her. Every day is a challenge. Through my behavior during the day, the things I do or say, I realize that Mary or Jesus would have done them differently—and better for sure. I am continuously making mistakes, tripping over my own ignorance, judgment, and self-centered ego. I have not yet fully conquered my ego.

Mary's Birth

After Her Immaculate Conception, Mary's birth was also special and supernatural. She was born from Anna in a completely different way from how humans are born. I summarize the accounts of Anne Catherine Emmerich that best explain it.

When the time came, Anna called three other women to help her with the delivery. She was expecting a normal delivery. Anna was kneeling before a cupboard in her room, when a supernatural light started filling the area. The light became more and more intense, completely surrounding Anna, who then stood up. The three women were so stunned that they sank to the ground. Then as Anna was reappearing from the intense light, she had the little baby in her hands, wrapped in her mantle and pressed to her heart.[6]

This inevitably brings us back to Eve and the Fall, when, after the original sin, God tells Eve that she will bear children in pain. Mary is the first human to be born in a supernatural way, without any pain for the mother. Jesus will later be born in the same way. Anne Catherine

6 *The Lowly*, I, 150–151

Emmerich states that all births would have been like Mary's, had it not been for the Fall.

We have established one important building block: Mary was conceived, immaculate, without sexual intercourse between Her parents, just like Jesus, the Son of God, would later be conceived. The Second Eternal Thought in the Blessing received by Joachim was incarnate in Anna, and Mary was conceived. Mary became the new Ark of the Covenant, carrying the First Eternal Thought in the Word—the Messiah.

Some of the bodies of the saints, who lived their lives close to the perfection of Mary and Jesus, have remained incorrupt. Saint Catherine Labouré, for example, died in 1876. When her body was exhumed fifty-six years later, it was unblemished. Her eyes were as blue as the day she died. Catherine Labouré can be seen today in the chapel of Rue du Bac 140 in Paris, and she still looks as though she only died yesterday. However, the bodies of Labouré and some other two hundred and fifty saints that remain incorrupt were not taken up with their spirits upon their death, like Mary's. It seems that this blessing is reserved only for the holiest.

It is quite interesting that at the time of Mary's birth, Anne Catherine Emmerich saw that there was great joy and agitation in nature and in the hearts of all good people. Birds were singing more than usual, and animals were playing. However, she also saw great fear and sorrow in sinners, and those who were possessed by evil spirits broke out into violent ravings and loud cries. Some of these cries were related to these evil spirits being unable to again enter men and torment them, because the announced Virgin that would crush the snake had been born.

A beautiful description of the Immaculate Conception is given by Jesus in the synagogue in Capernaum, in the discourse He made about "the bread which came down from heaven." [John 6:41] His audience is scandalized at His words. In her Poem, Maria Valtorta captures the following response of Jesus:

"Why are you grumbling among yourselves? Yes, I am the son of Mary of Nazareth, the daughter of Joachim of the house of David, a virgin consecrated in the Temple and then married to Joseph of Jacob, of the house of David. Many of you have known the just parents of Joseph, a royal carpenter, and those of Mary, the Virgin heiress of the royal stock. And you thus say: 'How can He say that he descended from Heaven?' and you become doubtful.

I remind you of the Prophets who prophesied the Incarnation of the Word. And I remind you that it is a dogma, more for us Israelites than for any other people, that He, Whose name we dare not mention, could not become Flesh according to the laws of mankind, and an impoverished mankind at that. The Most Pure Uncreated One, if he humiliated Himself by becoming Man for the sake of man, could but choose the womb of a Virgin purer than lilies to clothe His Divinity with Flesh. The Bread that descended from Heaven in the days of Moses, was placed in the gold Ark, which supported the Mercy Seat and was watched over by Cherubim, behind the veils of the Tabernacle. And the Word of God was with the Bread. And it was right that it should be so, because the deepest respect is to be paid to the gifts of God and to the tables of His most holy Word. So what will God have prepared for His own Word and for the true Bread that has come from Heaven? A more immaculate and precious Ark than the gold one, to support the precious Mercy Seat of His pure will to immolate Himself, watched over by the cherubim of God, veiled by virginal purity, by perfect humility, sublime charity and all the most holy virtues.

So? Do you not understand yet that My Paternity is in Heaven and that, consequently, I come from there?" [*The Poem*, III, 444-445]

The misunderstanding of the Immaculate Conception needs to be corrected. It needs to be better explained by the Church. There is so little education on the subject that even most Catholics don't really understand that it refers to Mary's conception, instead of Jesus' conception. Even in the book *Catechism of the Catholic Church*, there are only four paragraphs dedicated to the Immaculate Conception of Mary out of a total of 2,865 paragraphs.

Mary in Her apparitions presents Herself as the Mother of all, not just the Mother of Catholics. It seems to me that religious politics and pride have gotten in the way of Mary's true universality. Mary does not form part of our lives today. She is absent from the Church and everyday life. We have ignored Her because we knew not better. Man's pride has gotten in the way. Men have placed Mary in the closet and thrown away the key.

We need to bring Mary back into our lives; we have to let her fill some of the spaces in our hearts. We have been craving for a long time this loving motherly energy. We have been looking in so many places, without success, not knowing that our heart's desires could be fulfilled with Mary, who is right there for us. There is nothing like a mother when a child needs loving care. The union that exists between a mother and her child is so intimately special; it cannot be rivaled by any other relationship.

When I opened myself up to Mary, She came rushing in, like the torrents of the Niagara Falls, filling my heart with so much love and my life with so many blessings. Oh Mary, how sad it is that you had been there all these years, patiently waiting, put away and forgotten! How sad and painful it must have been for You, dear Mother, all these centuries, knowing that there was no place for You in human hearts.

Mary, You had to come as the light being You are and show Yourself to us in many places, so we would start noticing You, so we could find You again and bring You back to life. I thank You for these recent apparitions and for having eternal patience with us. I thank You for your loving presence and for making Yourself available to all of us, regardless of race or religion. It once was just one Christian faith; with You it can become just one faith again.

Pope John Paul II was one of the few recent Church magistrates who showed his strong devotion to Mary numerous times during his administration. Like Pope John Paul II, there are a few other Catholic authorities, including the current Pope Benedict XVI, who have a deep veneration for Mary. Several priests and Church authorities have investigated and written books on Mary. However, it still seems to me that in the Catholic Church institutions, Mariologists are a minority, and they have to swim against the current.

Religious practice in all faiths is mostly the product of centuries of male domination. From time immemorial, the various churches have been ruled by men, and women have had a secondary role. Times have changed, and thanks to the feminist movements, women now stand equal to man in almost every aspect of modern life. One of the few exceptions is still religion, where positions of authority continue to be widely assigned to men. Mary comes as a spiritual advocate for God for all humankind. She was never, and is certainly not now, interested in a position of authority.

It is time to open ourselves to the female wisdom and to the motherly love of Mary. Were it not for Her apparitions, we would not know Mary at all. Mary crushed the head of the snake when She incarnated and brought Jesus to life. Mary undid Eve's original sin through Her obedience and showed us a path back home, back to Paradise. But evil succeeded in shutting Her out soon after Her death, so sin could roam free in the world again. It is time to free Mary. It is time to crush the head of the snake again.

You may have noticed that there are hardly any songs composed to Mary playing in the radio these days. When you listen to Christian radio, you hear so many beautiful songs praising our Lord Jesus Christ. However, you hear nothing for Mary. This is strong evidence of how effective the imprisonment of Mary has been.

Few songs have the power of the Ave Maria, a glorious hymn to Mary. Or a more recent example, Paul McCartney and John Lennon's "Let it Be." When you listen carefully to the words and you let the song fill your heart, you cannot but conclude that Paul McCartney had a moment of divine inspiration when he composed this song. Mother Mary Herself must have touched his heart for this song to come to life. The lyrics talk about Mother Mary coming to us in times of trouble with words of wisdom and for us to "let it be".

The song reached number one in the United States and number two in the United Kingdom. In 2004, it was ranked number twenty on *Rolling Stone* magazine's list of the five hundred greatest songs of all time.[7] McCartney said "Let it Be" was inspired by a dream. Although he says the dream was of his mother, who died of cancer when he was fourteen, I believe that most people when they hear this song associate it with Mother Mary. It cuts across all ages and across all ethnic and religious groups. Perhaps you have already noticed that Mary said, "Behold the maidservant of the Lord! *Let it be* to me according to your word." [Luke 1:38]

The lyrics of the song: "Stairway to Heaven" by Led Zeppelin, "the heaviest band of all time" and "the biggest band of the 70s" according to *Rolling Stone* magazine, is also quite impressive.

> ...And as we wind on down the road
> Our shadows taller than our souls
> There walks a lady we all know
> Who shines white light and wants to show

When I read all the lyrics of this song, my eyes get watery and my throat gets tight because I can feel how Mary could have been talking to Robert Plant, the vocalist of the group who wrote them. Here is what Plant said: "My hand was writing out the words, '*There's a lady is sure, all that glitters is gold, and she's buying a stairway to heaven.*' I just sat there and looked at them and almost leapt out of my seat."

This song was never released as a single, but as an album it had sold 23 million copies in the United States alone by July 31, 2006. It is one of the 100 Greatest Rock Songs and it is the most requested and most played song on FM radio stations in the United States.[8]

How can it be that a rock band can get this type of inspiration? In a part of the song it says instead of rock and roll, we have "to be rocks

---

7 Let it Be. In Wikipedia. Retrieved August 23, 2008, from http://en.wikipedia.org/wiki/Let_it_be

8 Stairway to Heaven. In Wikipedia. Retrieved August 23, 2008, from http://en.wikipedia.org/wiki/Stairway_to_Heaven

and not roll." And in another, that if we listen hard, a tune will come to us at last, when "all is one and one is all." Did Robert Plant, a musician I greatly admire, know what he was writing when he composed this song? What is it with music, that it touches your soul so deeply? Is it the effect of the inspired words? The vibrations between the music and the words? I don't know, but what would we be without music?

The end result is that "Let it Be" is one of the greatest songs of all time; the same is true of Robert Plant's song "Stairway to Heaven." This is a testimony to Her universality. Mary can unify us and help us forget our differences. Mary can bring an end to war, if we allow Her...if we let Her be part of our lives, and if we listen and follow Her advice.

During the cold war, when John F. Kennedy was battling Nikita Khrushchev, the president of the Soviet Union at the time, for the removal of nuclear missiles from Cuba, the world was on the verge of a nuclear confrontation. Those were days of extreme tension. The possibility of a third world war was very high. At the same time, Mary was appearing to three children in Garabandal, Spain. Author John Kirby, in his work "The Affect of Higher Intelligences on Events in the Early 1960s" associates the presence of Mary in the world at this precise time as key to averting the war and helping find a peaceful solution.

The cover of this book is a painting that hangs in my bedroom. I can see it directly in front of me from my bed, and I love to watch it when praying the rosary. We purchased it from the artist, Raisa Goltsin, who lives in South Florida. Beatriz and I liked this painting because it portrays Mary in the light of the Universal Mother, as the Caretaker of the Earth. Raisa was kind enough to give me permission to use it as the cover of this book. To me, this painting portrays the return of Mary, the resurrection of Mary for all mankind.

Mary was announced by God from the beginning of time; for centuries Her coming was prepared for. She finally came to life in complete purity, "full of grace," in an immaculate way, as Eve was before the Fall; She became the New Ark of the Covenant, the vessel in which the

Son of God was to become incarnate. The Messiah could now be born "doubly immaculate." The temple in which He was to reside until His birth was the most pure possible, and worthy of Him, the Son of God.

Chapter 6

The Annunciation and Virginal Conception

Mary was a precocious girl and a fast learner. By age three, She could already read and have intelligent conversations with adults. Mary wanted to enter the Temple and serve God since the very beginning. She could conceive no other life path for Herself, and She was anxious to begin sooner rather than later. Because of Her accelerated development and desires, Anna and Joachim decided to allow Mary to enter the Temple services at age three. This was earlier than usual for the children.[1]

Sending a child to the Temple was no simple decision, since it meant not seeing your child, except maybe once a year. Parents gave parental rights regarding the upbringing of a child to the priests in the Temple. I can't imagine how difficult this decision must have been for Anna and Joachim, who had been waiting for this child for so long, only to see her go just a few years later.

The process of entering the Temple in service of God was no simple task either. The child had to be accepted by the priests in the Temple.

1 *The Lowly*, I, 156

The priests would thoroughly evaluate the child through a set of questions to determine if the child had the wisdom and the proper spirit for Temple service.

Mary was so smart that She not only properly answered all the questions She was subjected to, but She went beyond the requirements. For example, Mary said that once in the Temple She would follow a more strict food diet than what was required, because this was the way in which She would show Her sacrifice to God. Upon hearing this, Joachim begged his daughter to please not take on such a harsh sacrifice. However, the child Mary was so happy to be entering the Temple that for Her it did not seem like a sacrifice.

Throughout the eleven years She was in the Temple, Mary lived a happy life dedicated to prayer and service to God. Among other duties, She had to handwash clothes, including the garments of the priests. During all this time Mary had no clue that She was to become the mother of the Messiah. To the contrary, She was committed to living a virginal life fully dedicated to God in the Temple. Her greatest desire was to see the birth of the Messiah, which had been announced, and possibly to help the mother of this child in any capacity.

At age fourteen, Mary was approached by the priests in the Temple and told that She had to leave the Temple and marry. This was the proper thing to do for Her at this time, since there was the strong belief that the Messiah was to come from one of the descendants of the virgins in the Temple. Mary was devastated; She could not believe that She was being asked to leave the Temple, much less believe that She was being asked to marry.

Mary had no interest in men and could not see Herself married to any man. She prayed to God to spare Her from this. She felt marriage would separate Her from God. Mary felt that leaving the Temple was the wrong thing to do. Her only desire was to remain a virgin, with Her life dedicated to God.

Despite Her pleas, a proper husband was sought for Mary. Once again the priests did what had been done before with Her mother and Her ancestors; suitors were asked to bring a branch to the Temple. Each suitor had to write his name on the branch. The branch that flowered would belong to Mary's future husband. Many suitors came with their branches, but none flourished.

The priests then searched the records to see if any descendant of David was missing. They found that one from Bethlehem had not shown up. It was Joseph, who had renounced married life for devotion to God and thus had not participated. However, on command of the high priest, Joseph came to the Temple with his branch. As he was about to lay his branch in front of the Holy of Holies, the branch flowered, bringing forth a beautiful lily.

Joseph, the man chosen to become the husband of Mary, was a devout Jew, much older than Mary at age thirty, who had led an exemplary life. His father was called Jacob and Jacob's parents lived in a large house outside Bethlehem, once the ancestral home of King David, whose father Jesse had owned it. This is the same Jesse of the prophecy of Isaiah that said Mary would come from the branch of the tree of Jesse. [Isaiah 11:1]

When Mary and Joseph met, Joseph quickly gave Mary the peace of mind She needed. He told Her that he would respect Her desire to remain virgin. Neither Joseph nor Mary had any idea that the Messiah was to be born to them. Mary's mother, Anna, knew that Mary was to be the mother of the Messiah. The angel that told her she was going to conceive Mary told her to keep this secret to herself.

Mary and Joseph started their married life in Nazareth, where they lived in a house that belonged to Anna. Joseph worked as a carpenter, while Mary tended the house and the garden. She dedicated much time to the garden, where She grew various plants and flowers. Her favorite flowers were lilies of the valley. Anne Catherine Emmerich explains that Mary would spend hours in the garden in a state of introspection, prayer, and meditation. Joseph was an earthly, practical man, while Mary was very much a heavenly, spiritual woman. They both complemented each other in their different ways.

Meditation

I have mentioned in previous chapters that it is important to find time to quiet the mind and to learn by ourselves what God's will for us is. I am sure that Mary was able to keep Her purity and perfection because She stayed in permanent communication with God. In Her prayers and meditations, She must have found that place where you are one with God.

The first thing needed for effective meditation is an open mind. Deepak Chopra's books had a profound influence on my understanding of Eastern techniques and meditation. They helped my rational mind find a reasonable explanation for why these approaches worked. Chopra is an M.D. specializing in neurology, a field that studies the human nervous system, of which the brain is a major part. Chopra helped me understand the concept of what he calls "the field of pure potentiality," and how we can use our own capabilities to access a place of divine inspiration, where everything is possible.

Wayne Dyer, another great author I highly recommend, talks about intention and inspiration in his books and the role that these actions have in creating the life we want for ourselves. When we are clear about our life intentions and we bring these intentions forward in the quiet of our mind, we use our free will to create the future we want. If our intentions are for our highest good, the field of pure potentiality, as Chopra calls it, will manifest our desires. I would add that if our intentions, or our free will, are in synchrony with God's will, they will manifest quickly.

Meditation has allowed me to synchronize my free will with my spirit, and at times this internal voice can be surprisingly "loud and clear." One time when I was meditating, a loud masculine voice suddenly started speaking to me from about three feet to the left of my body. I felt such bliss with this presence next to me that I was fearful of opening my eyes and losing that wonderful feeling. My curiosity, however, won, and I looked over my left shoulder, sure there was someone there, but I could not see anything. The message I received, though, was very relevant to my life at that particular point.

During meditation I have also received visual images, concepts, and ideas that I have later put into practice with good results. I now consult God about all my major decisions while in meditation and prayer. I find a place where there is silence and where I know I will not be interrupted, ideally the same place each time. Then I sit down comfortably, with my legs crossed, and I try to keep my back as straight as I can. You must be comfortable to be able to meditate.

I then become aware of my breathing and try to take some deep breaths, while I do my prayers. I visualize my energy centers and focus individually on each one of them, starting from the lower one and moving slowly up. Once I feel that my body is relaxed and open to divine intervention, I visualize my spirit moving out of my body and meeting Mary in Heaven. Then I merge or fuse my spiritual body with that of Mary, becoming one with Her. After this, both of our bodies merge or fuse with God, becoming one with Him and thereby with all creation. At this point I imagine myself being here, there, and everywhere, reaching all the confines of the universe.

I stay in this state of connection with the divine for as long as I can, trying to keep my mind free from any other ideas and using my breath to help me focus. Sometimes it is easy, and other times it is more difficult, depending on the distracting things that may be going on in my life and preoccupations or other ideas that steal my attention. When a random thought appears, I just acknowledge it, accept it, and then go back as quickly as I can to my point of stillness.

Most times when I am in this meditative state, I do not receive any ideas or messages, but other times I get important messages. Specifically, when I meditate asking for direction, I usually get a response the first time, provided the conditions are appropriate for concentration and stillness. Each person who meditates does something different; in fact, I think each person should work on his or her own technique, whatever works best.

I think that it is important to meditate at least once a day for at least twenty or thirty minutes. Aside from the well-known benefits to your physical body's health, which have been documented by scientist, you will be able to connect with that space that Chopra calls the field of pure potentiality, where in my opinion you can discover what God's will is for you in this life.

Mary practiced meditation, as did Jesus. Here is what Maria Valtorta recorded about a conversation the risen Christ had with the Apostles about meditation:

> "And is meditation not the most active prayer? And have I not made you contemplate and meditate and have I not given a subject on which to meditate since I met you on the road, moving your hearts with true acts of holy feelings? This is prayer, men: to get in touch with the Eternal and with the things that help to lead the spirit far beyond the Earth, and from the meditation on the perfections of God and the miseries of man, of one's ego, rouse acts of a will, which is either loving or repairing, but always adoring, even if it is a will rising from meditation on a fault or a punishment. Evil and good serve for the final purpose, if one knows how to make use of them. I have told you many a time." [*The Poem*, V, 772–773]

Perhaps for Christian followers, an important aspect of this discussion is that meditation is a great complement to your spiritual development. There is a paradigm that if you are Christian, you do not follow Eastern spiritual practices. In my humble opinion, this wrong paradigm needs to be eliminated. The path to enlightenment can be aided by embracing techniques and practices that have proven over centuries to open our spirits and shut down our minds, so we can hear God more clearly.

The Annunciation

The Church celebrates the Annunciation, when Archangel Gabriel appeared to Mary to announce She would be the mother of the Messiah, on March 25th. Luke's Gospel talks about the annunciation in full detail:

> And in the sixth month the angel Gabriel was sent from God unto a city of Galilee, named Nazareth, To a virgin espoused to a man whose name was Joseph, of the house of David; and the virgin's name was Mary. And the angel came in unto her, and said, Hail, thou that art highly favoured, the Lord is with thee: blessed art thou among women. And when she saw him, she was troubled at his saying, and cast in her mind what manner of salutation this should be. And the angel said unto her, Fear not, Mary: for thou hast found favour with God. And, behold, thou shalt conceive in thy womb, and bring forth a son, and shalt call his name JESUS. He shall be great, and shall be called the Son of the Highest: and the Lord God shall give unto him the throne of his father David: And he shall reign over the house of Jacob for ever; and of his kingdom there shall be no end. Then said Mary unto the angel, How shall this be, seeing I know not a man? And the angel answered and said unto her, The Holy Ghost shall come upon thee, and the power of the Highest shall overshadow thee: therefore also that holy thing which shall be born of thee shall be called the Son of God. And, behold, thy cousin Elisabeth, she hath also conceived a son in her old age: and this is the sixth month with her, who was called barren. For *with God nothing shall be impossible.* And Mary said, Behold the handmaid of the Lord; be it unto me according to thy word. And the angel departed from her. [Luke 1:26–38]

Anne Catherine Emmerich, through her visions, provides greater detail about how this event took place. She explains that Mary was in their house in Nazareth, soon after Her marriage, with Her mother Anna, who was visiting. Mary's father, Joachim, had already died by the time that Mary married, and Anna had remarried. With Mary were two other girls about her age and Anna's cousin. Because of Anna's wealthy situation, she was able to provide many of the things that Mary and Joseph lacked, and the whole house had been newly fitted for them. They were all busy arranging these new things during the day.[2]

---

2 *The Lowly*, I, 193

In the evening, after eating, they separated. Mary went into her bedchamber. She put on a long white woolen praying robe and covered her head with a yellowish white veil. She knelt down and prayed fervently for a long time, with her face raised to Heaven. Suddenly, at around midnight, a mass of light started coming from the ceiling of the room and landed at her right side. In this shining light was a young youth, with flowing yellow hair. It was the Angel Gabriel.

> The angel, with hands gently raised before his breast, spoke to Mary. I saw the words like letters of glittering light issuing from his lips. Mary replied, but without looking up. Then the angel again spoke and Mary, as if in obedience to his command, raised her veil a little, glanced at him, and said: "Behold the handmaid of the Lord. May it be done unto me according to thy word." ...As Mary uttered the words...I saw an apparition of the Holy Ghost. The countenance was human, and the whole apparition environed by dazzling splendor, as if surrounded by wings. From the breast and hands, I saw issuing three streams of light. They penetrated the right side of the Blessed Virgin and united into one under her heart. At that instant Mary became perfectly transparent and luminous. It was as if opacity disappeared like darkness before that flood of light.
>
> While the angel and with him the streams of glory vanished, I saw down the path of light that led up to heaven, showers of half-brown roses and tiny green leaves falling upon Mary. She, entirely absorbed in self, saw in herself the Incarnate Son of God, a tiny, human form of light with all its members, even the little fingers perfect. It was about midnight that I saw this mystery. [*The Lowly*, I, 195]

After the angel disappeared, Mary, who was enveloped in a deep ecstasy, knew that She had conceived the Messiah, the Son of the Most High. God was now in His Temple. When Mary said, "Behold the handmaid of the Lord, be it done to me according to thy word," the Word entered into Her, taking possession of His Temple. Mary was now the Temple and the New Ark of the Covenant. At this point

Anna with the other women came into Mary's room because there was great commotion in nature, and a cloud of light had appeared above the house. Anna was also given the grace of interior knowledge, so she knew what had happened.

It was God's will for this child to be born from Mary's womb after nine months and not just appear as a perfect and beautiful newly created being. God had already done that once with Adam, and he *disobeyed*. God this time did not take any shortcuts and prepared the way for Mary over many generations, so She could be the Mother of the Messiah. Jesus did not come sooner because until then no other creature had achieved the purity that was required. There was no one who could become the New Ark of the Covenant, the Temple worthy of God, where He could comfortably reside.

We can now begin to understand better all God's efforts to preserve the ancestry line of Jesus, to protect them from other people inhabiting earth. God's direction to Joshua when he was entering the Promised Land was to kill the people of the towns they would conquer, so that they would not marry with other races or peoples and the newly established Israelite religion would survive.

There was no way in which the Israelites from Abraham to Mary would have survived without God's protection. If there was one common practice during the several thousand years before Christ, it was that conquerors would completely destroy conquered cities and towns. It was customary to kill all the people you conquered. In those times, supremacy was feeble and it was just a matter of time before your turn would arrive. Even of the twelve tribes of Israel, only two had survived by 150 BC.: the tribes of Judah and Benjamin

A couple of other major problems of the time were human sacrifices and sexual intercourse between humans and animals. We have to remember that during these times, non-Israelites would sacrifice their own children to their gods. Some of the rituals of sacrifice at the time were terribly sinister. In terms of sexual intercourse with animals, it must have been a common practice of the time for the Law of Moses to completely prohibit this. Otherwise, why would it be mentioned?

It is from this world of complete havoc that the Messiah was to come. How would this be possible if not by isolating a group of people, nurturing them, caring for them, and protecting them as God did? How could the Essenes, the ancestors of Mary, have achieved such a high level of spiritual development if not for the fact that they evolved from one of twelve tribes of Israel and descended from the house of Judah, directly from king David?

Perhaps in this historical context, we can now understand some parts of the Old Testament and gain perspective of its sometimes vengeful and punishing God—definitively not the God with which most of us identify now.

The implication for mankind of Mary's obedience is huge. For the first time since the creation of man, a human being lived in perfect *obedience* to God. With Her commitment and Her perfect life, Mary became the pure vessel of grace promised by God to mankind, the mother of the Incarnate Word from the beginning of time.

Mary's perfect and *obedient* life would not have been possible without Her Immaculate Conception, which eliminated a great part of sinful human nature. Her Immaculate Conception, in turn, would have not been possible without the purification of Her ancestry line, which finally made Mary's parents worthy of the Word of God preserved in the Ark of the Covenant by the Israelites.

At the same time, Jesus conception was a "second" Immaculate Conception, making Him doubly pure. It would not have been possible for Jesus to do what He did had He not been conceived in this absolutely pure way, with all the "Godly" material He needed for His mission. Only Mary and Jesus were thus born in the condition of "full of grace," the condition that Eve and Adam had enjoyed before the Fall.

While Eve and Adam *disobeyed* God, Mary and Jesus *obeyed* God perfectly and always, and in doing so they undid Eve and Adam's sin. Mary, the female aspect of humanity, came first and annulled the fault of the first sinner—Eve. Jesus came next, the male aspect of humanity, annulling Adam's sin and finalizing the Redemption of humankind.

Mary and Jesus are the first two humans on Earth able to control their free will and use it for their benefit to transcend beyond this physical plane. In doing this, they have shown us the way. They have become a living example of what it is to seek the perfection of God.

When Mary said, "*Let it be* to me according to your word" [Luke 1:38] She had the choice of saying no. Her free will allowed Her to say no. But in Her perfect *obedience* to God, She chose to say yes, as She had done since Her birth. In fact, Maria Valtorta explains that all the heavens were nervously awaiting Mary's response, because to them it was not a done a deal that Mary would say yes. Had Mary said no, the Redemption of mankind would have been again delayed, who knows until when.

This seemingly simple act was indeed quite complicated, because Mary not only received the happy news of conceiving the son of God. She also received the sad news of how difficult this journey was going to be and how much She was to suffer because of the Messiah. Moreover, Mary took the risk of being stoned to death if the news were misinterpreted by Joseph and the people in Nazareth. It was customary at the time to stone a woman who was unfaithful to her husband.

Up to this point, only Anna had been granted the grace of knowing that the Word had Incarnated in Mary and that it was God's desire to keep this secret. Some days later, when Joseph returned home to Nazareth, Mary did not tell him anything. Although She wanted to tell Joseph, She kept God's secret with great humility.

Mary asked Joseph to take Her to visit Her cousin Elizabeth, because She had learned from the angel that Elizabeth was now six months' pregnant with child, and Mary had a great desire to visit her. Elizabeth was married to Zacharias, and they lived in Jutta, near Hebron, a few days' journey from Nazareth.

The Visitation

Zacharias and Elizabeth were much older than Joseph and Mary. Zacharias was a priest in the Temple; Angel Gabriel appeared to him and told him that his wife Elizabeth was going to conceive a child, to be called John, who would precede the Messiah. [Luke 1:11–20] This child was later to become John the Baptist. Zacharias did not believe this, as his wife was old and barren, so the Angel told him he would lose his voice until John was born.

When Mary arrived at Zacharias' house and greeted Elizabeth in what is described as "The Visitation," the baby in Elizabeth's womb immediately felt the presence of the Lord in Mary's womb.

> And it came to pass, that, when Elisabeth heard the salutation of Mary, the babe leaped in her womb; and Elisabeth was filled with the Holy Ghost: And she spake out with a loud voice, and said, Blessed art thou among women, and blessed is the fruit of thy womb. And whence is this to me, that the mother of my Lord should come to me? For, lo, as soon as the voice of thy salutation sounded in mine ears, the babe leaped in my womb for joy. And blessed is she that believed: for there shall be a performance of those things which were told her from the Lord. [Luke 1:41–45]

After this Mary started singing the Magnificat, also known as the Song of Mary, which has its origins in this Visitation. The Magnificat is a canticle frequently sung or spoken liturgically in Christian church services, including Roman Catholic, Anglican, and Protestant. The Magnificat is an expression of gratitude to God for the fulfillment of the blessing and promises to the Israelites. The text of the canticle is taken directly from the Gospel of Luke [Luke 1:46–55] and is now used for common worship in the following way:

> **The Magnificat**
> My soul doth magnify the Lord,
> And my spirit hath rejoiced in God my Saviour.
> For he hath regarded the low estate of his handmaiden
> for, behold, from henceforth all generations shall call me
> blessed.
> For he that is mighty hath done to me great things;
> and holy is his name.
> And his mercy is on them that fear him from generation
> to generation.

> He hath shewed strength with his arm;
> he hath scattered the proud in the imagination of their
> hearts.
> He hath put down the mighty from their seats,
> and exalted them of low degree.
> He hath filled the hungry with good things;
> and the rich he hath sent empty away.
> He hath helped his servant Israel, in remembrance of his
> mercy;
> As he spake to our fathers, to Abraham,
> and to his seed for ever. [Luke 1:46–55]

When you ponder about what just happened to Mary, when She received recognition from Elizabeth, you cannot but think about Her great humility. Any other human being, especially at this young age of fourteen, would have thought herself special and maybe taken some personal claim to be the chosen one. But Mary in Her most humble attitude does not say a word to Elizabeth but starts to recite the Magnificat.

The first thing Mary does is proclaim the greatness of God and how She is saved by Him. She then refers to Herself as "his lowly servant," not as somebody who has worked hard at earning the attention and recognition of God. We will see this humility in Mary throughout Her life, despite knowing for a fact that She conceived the greatest human being ever. Quite admirable, when you think about it.

From a historical point of view, since the beginning of Christianity, people believed in the Virginal Conception of Jesus. Many early writings from the apostles and Church Fathers confirmed this, and established faith confirmed it as well. There were a few challenges to the Virginal Conception in early Christianity, before the fourth century, by some thinkers, but these were dismissed by the Church. After those early challenges, there have not been any more formal challenges to this doctrine that the Church has had to rebuke.

Back in 431 AD, the Ecumenical Council of Ephesus (modern

day Turkey) was called to debate about the controversial teachings of Nestorius, bishop of Constantinople. In this Council of Ephesus, it was decreed that Mary was Theotokos (Greek word for God-bearer, or the one who gives birth to God) because Her son Jesus is one person who is both God and man, divine and human.[3]

The Virginal Conception of Jesus was not challenged. Nestorius asked how Jesus, being part man, could not be partially a sinner as well, since man is by definition a sinner since the Fall. In this Council, Nestorius' position was defeated. Not only was Mary confirmed as God-bearer, but the Virginal Conception was also ratified.

Actually, today all the various Christian church denominations accept the Virginal Conception of Jesus. What may differ from one denomination to another is how Mary is venerated. The Catholic faith is the most active in the veneration of Mary.

The Virginal Conception of Jesus is not the same as Mary's Perpetual Virginity, which is how the Catholic faith now defines this dogma. The Perpetual Virginity of Mary includes the Virginal Conception of Jesus, but also establishes that Mary remained virgin until her death. This is where Christian church denominations differ. We shall review this later, after the birth of Jesus and the subject of whether Mary had other children or not.

Mary and Elizabeth did not tell Joseph and Zacharias anything about Mary's pregnancy. Joseph returned to Nazareth, while Mary stayed with Elizabeth for three months until after the birth of John the Baptist. Zacharias, as announced by the angel, miraculously recovered his voice during the circumcision of John. [Luke 1:63]

Eventually Mary had to go back to her home in Nazareth Three months' pregnant, She had to face Joseph. What would She tell him? How would she explain Her condition? Would he believe Her? These thoughts must have troubled Mary quite a bit along the journey.

Joseph was deeply troubled by Mary's condition when he saw Her.

3 Theotokos. In Wikipedia. Retrieved August 24, 2008 from http://en.wikipedia.org/wiki/Theotokos

He knew nothing of the Annunciation, because Mary was still keeping God's secret.

> Her husband Joseph, being an upright man and wanting to spare her disgrace, decided to divorce her informally. He had made up his mind to do this when suddenly the angel of the Lord appeared to him in a dream and said, "Joseph, son of David, do not be afraid to take Mary home as your wife, because she has conceived what is in her by the Holy Spirit. She will give birth to a son and you must name him Jesus, because he is the one who is to save his people from their sins." Now all this took place to fulfill what the Lord had spoken through the prophet:
>
> Look! The virgin is with child and will give birth to a son whom they will call Immanuel, a name which means 'God-is-with-us'. When Joseph woke up he did what the angel of the Lord had told him to do; he took his wife to his home; he had not had intercourse with her when she gave birth to a son; and he named him Jesus. [Matthew 1:19–25 NJB]

In Maria Valtorta's writings, we hear Mary's words describing the difficult moments She had, which She calls Her first Passion. She felt a deep torment in Her soul, because She could not concede to Joseph what had happened with the Angel of God:

> "Oh! Our first Passion! Who can feel its intimate and silent intensity? Who can describe My pain when I realized that Heaven had not yet heard My prayer by revealing the mystery to Joseph?
>
> I understood that he was not aware of it when I saw that he was respectful to me as usual. If he had known that I bore in Me the Word of God, he would have adored that Word enclosed in My womb, with the acts of veneration which are due to God and which he would not have failed to accomplish, as I would not have refused to receive, not for My own sake, but for Him Who was within Me and that I bore, as the Ark of Alliance carried the stone code and vases of manna..."

"...Who can truly tell Joseph's pain, his thoughts, the perturbation of his feelings? Like a little boat caught in a great storm, he was in a vortex of conflicting ideas, in a turmoil of reflections, of which one was more piercing and painful than the other. He was, to all appearances, a man betrayed by his wife. He saw his good reputation and the esteem of his world collapse around him; because of Her he saw scornful fingers pointed at himself and felt pitied by the village people. Above all, he perceived that his love and esteem for Me had fallen, struck to death, before the evidence of a deed.

In this respect, his holiness shines brighter than Mine. And I give this witness with the affection of a spouse, because I want you to love My Joseph, this wise, prudent, patient and good man, who is not separated from the mystery of Redemption, on the contrary, he is closely connected to it, because he suffered for it, consuming himself in sorrow for it, saving your Saviour at the cost of his own sacrifice because of his holiness.

Had he not been so holy, he would have acted in a human way, denouncing Me as an adulteress so that I should be stoned... But Joseph was holy. His pure spirit lived in God." [*The Poem*, I, 124–125]

"If God had not said to Me: 'Be silent!' I would probably have dared say to Joseph, with My face bowed to the ground: 'The Spirit has penetrated Me and now the Embryo of God is in Me,' and he would have believed Me, because he held Me in high esteem and because like those who never lie, he could not believe that others lied. Yes, to avoid hurting his feelings in future, I would have overcome My reluctance to praise Myself. But I obeyed the divine command. And for months after that moment, I felt the first wound pierced My heart." [*The Poem*, I, 94]

When Joseph finally learned the truth of Mary's pregnancy, he asked Mary to forgive him for wanting to leave Her. Here is what Mary answered and how the conversation with Joseph went:

> "I have nothing for which to forgive you. On the contrary, I ask you to forgive Me for the pain I caused you." [Mary says]
>
> "Oh! Yes, it was a great pain! What a torture! Look! I was told this morning that my temples are white-haired and my face wrinkled. These past days have been more than ten years of my life! But why, Mary, have You been so humble as to conceal Your glory from me, Your spouse, and thus allow me to suspect You?" Joseph is not on his knees, but he is bent so low that he is as good as kneeling down, and Mary lays Her tiny hand on his head and smiles. She seems to be absolving him. And She whispers: "If I had not been humble in the most perfect manner, I would not have deserved to conceive the Expected One, Who is coming to pay for the sin of pride that ruined man. And then I obeyed...God had requested such obedience. It cost Me so much...because of you, because of the pain that you were to suffer. But I could but obey. I am the Handmaid of the Lord, and servants do not discuss the orders they receive. They fulfill them, Joseph, even if they cause bitter tears." Mary weeps quietly while speaking. So quietly that Joseph, bent down as he is, does not notice it until a tear falls on the floor.
>
> He then lifts his head and—it is the first time I see him do this—he presses Mary's little hands in his dark strong ones and he kisses the tips of the rosy slender fingers that protrude like fresh buds of a peach-tree from the circle formed by his own hands. [*The Poem*, I, 127]

Luckily for all of us, Mary said yes to the Holy Spirit, and Joseph accepted the miraculous conception. Both obediently accepted God's will and allowed the course of history to bring the Redemption to mankind, with no further delays.

Chapter 7

God's Timing

Life proceeded normally for Mary once Joseph was made aware that Mary was to bear the Messiah. They lived in Nazareth throughout this time. Jesus would have been born in Nazareth had it not been for the angel of God who appeared to Joseph and told him to take off at once with Mary to Bethlehem, because the child was to be born there.

This part of Mary's life is detailed in the accounts of Anne Catherine Emmerich, which I summarize here.

The angel explained they should take only basic necessities and that they should take two animals, the donkey upon which Mary was to ride on and another one-year-old female donkey. The female donkey was to run free, and they should follow whatever path it took. At the time, King Herod had declared a census and required that all inhabitants should register in their corresponding birth town, so a lot of people were traveling back and forth. Joseph had planned to do this after the birth of the baby; Mary was well into her ninth month of pregnancy and a trip this long would not be good for Her.

The next day Joseph and Mary packed what was necessary for

the trip and started off on a trip of ten days. Once more, it is hard to imagine that Mary and Joseph did not question God's will, despite the absurd timing of God's request. It was a difficult trip because Mary was at the end of Her nine month of pregnancy. She would walk and ride the donkey, but they had to make many stops to rest. The young female donkey chose roads that were not necessarily the fastest or the easiest routes to Bethlehem.

As they approached Bethlehem, Mary's pregnancy was coming to completion, and She knew there was not much time left. Joseph reassured Mary that they would find a proper place for Her to give birth because he knew many people in Bethlehem. After all, it was his native town. He was sure of being able to get help. Upon entering the city, Joseph went house by house asking for help, explaining that his wife was about to give birth, but no one lent them a hand. It was God's will for this baby to be born in the utmost simplicity and not in a house.

Finally, after many attempts and in much frustration, Joseph decided to take Mary to a cave that he knew from his infancy. The cave was large enough to accommodate Mary in one area and for Joseph to make accommodations for himself in another. After making sure he had left Mary in the best possible way with what was available to them in the cave, Joseph went to town to look for a maidservant. At this point Mary was ready to give birth.

It was night, and Mary was kneeling, engaged in prayer, when a ray of light started descending to Her from a hole that had been opened in the top of the cave. The ray of light shot from the sky and illuminated the whole area, engulfing Mary. The maidservant and Joseph kneeled as they saw this miracle happen and started blessing God. Mary stood up and the light completely surrounded Her for a while. After the light started to dissipate, Mary was carrying the baby in Her hands.[1]

It was definitively a different way of giving birth. Maria Valtorta's visions of the birth of Jesus are practically identical.

---

1 *The Lowly*, I, Page 226

> And the light increases more and more. It is now unbearable to the eye. And the Virgin disappears in so much light, as if She had been absorbed by an incandescent curtain...and the Mother emerges.
>
> Yes. When the light becomes endurable once again to my eyes, I see Mary with the new-born Son in Her arms. [*The Poem*, I, 140]

In Anne Catherine Emmerich's and Maria Valtorta's descriptions, Jesus is born in a supernatural way, just as Mary was born of Anna. Mary's virginity was thus preserved after the birth of Jesus. This is referred to as the Virgin Birth of Jesus.

From faraway lands, people who studied the stars had also been watching the sky and had reached the conclusion that their prophecies were about to be fulfilled. A child was to be born from a virgin, and this child would become the most powerful king on Earth and would lead men closer to God. In three different kingdoms, three separate kings started off on a journey to follow the shinning star and bring presents and praise the newborn king. This unusual astronomical event must have been very significant and visible to all, but probably only those who studied the stars could recognize the significance of the event.

The three wise men followed the star that led them for many weeks directly to the cave of nativity in Bethlehem. When they arrived, the three wise men could not be more surprised. They were expecting to arrive at a palace, worthy of a king, not a cave. But they quickly understood that this was the will of God, and that this child had to be born in the most humble way.

After delivering their presents to the newborn king and honoring both parents, the three wise men spent the night in their campsite. They knew they could not remain there, because an angel had warned them of King Herod's intentions if they returned by way of Jerusalem. They left early the next day by a different road, to avoid going through Jerusalem.

King Herod had been waiting for the three wise men to return and inform him where the newborn child was, but when he realized that they were not coming back, he was furious. He ordered his Roman troops to kill all male children under two years old. But the angel of God once again appeared to Joseph and told him that he should leave Bethlehem immediately and go to Egypt, where the child would be safe.

> And when they were departed, behold, the angel of the Lord appeareth to Joseph in a dream, saying, Arise, and take the young child and his mother, and flee into Egypt, and be thou there until I bring thee word: for Herod will seek the young child to destroy him. When he arose, he took the young child and his mother by night, and departed into Egypt: And was there until the death of Herod: that it might be fulfilled which was spoken of the Lord by the prophet, saying, Out of Egypt have I called my son. [Matthew 2:13–15]

I cannot but be amazed at the *obedience* of Joseph and Mary. What mother would have accepted taking a trip right before giving birth and then again with a newborn baby? They knew that the trip to Egypt was a long one. It was not like going to a nearby town. This trip would take many more days than the trip to Bethlehem. Still they did as the angel of God had ordered. It was God's will.

In the case of the trip from Nazareth to Bethlehem, Mary and Joseph had to leave at once carrying only a few simple things. In the case of the trip to Egypt, they also left with nothing except what was left of the gifts of the wise men that they had not already given away in charity.

The slaughtering of the children of Israel is something that is typically remembered by most people, even those without much religious education. It is hard to envision such a cruel measure by King Herod. But it did take place, and many children were killed. John the Baptist, who at the time was six months older than Jesus, was taken into the wilderness by his mother who received a message sent by Mary and Joseph. Because of Zacharias' high position in Israel, King Herod believed the promised child could be his, and he was persecuted by the Romans and eventually killed for not revealing where Elizabeth had gone with the baby.[2]

Elizabeth and little John also received divine help while in the wilderness. After many days, Elizabeth returned to her home to find Zacharias dead, but John stayed in the wild and grew up in nature, with the animals. He wore sheep skin and ate what nature provided. His mother would come and visit him often, and he would go into town to visit his mother every now and then. But always he would return to live his life in the solitude of nature. As we know, later John started baptizing people with water in the Jordan River, preparing the way for Jesus' mission.

I always wonder what would have happened if Mary and Joseph had stayed in Nazareth. Notice how miracles occur when God's will is followed, although our lives will not be free of hardships. I can recall an instance when I had such a calling and did not follow God's will immediately. It happened on November 30, 2007. I was already living in Sedona and traveling to Miami frequently to attend to business.

The year of 2007 was a year of many changes in my life. As I mentioned earlier, the wind of change had begun in 2006, when Beatriz and I felt God's calling to move out of Miami, which eventually led us to Sedona. I had also felt the need to leave my work and an urge to move on with God's will for me in my life, which was to write this book. I had decided to offer my resignation at the end of June 2008.

But I was not listening carefully to God. My timing was not His timing. In November 2007, the wind of change became a sudden tornado. Just like tornados that can come out of nowhere and leave a path of destruction, I had an experience that certainly pushed me into making changes in my life sooner than June 2008.

On the night of November 30th I had a major car accident that

---

2 *The Lowly*, I, 320

almost cost me my life—probably did cost me my life, but I was given another chance. I was driving back home late at night from the Phoenix airport, after a long flight from Miami. It had been a tiring week. I had traveled to our office in Brazil, flown back Thursday night, worked all Friday at the Miami office, and then flown to Phoenix late that afternoon.

I was listening to a program on Christian radio that talked about "letting go and letting God." It explained that while we may think we have placed our lives in the hands of God, in reality we probably have not. We do the things we want to do, instead of the things that God wants us to do. The message in this program resonated. I had been trying all these years to do just that, to listen to God. But as I listened to the program I realized how far I still was from this goal.

At the end of the program there was a short prayer, where we were asked to repeat aloud our promise to let God really take charge of our lives. I did the prayer with a heart full of desire, but at the same time thought to myself, 'Oh, what I am getting into? What pleasant or unpleasant surprises will this prayer bring to me?' Following God's will is not an easy path. It is "the road less traveled."

About just three minutes later and without any apparent cause, I lost control of my Toyota Tundra pickup truck. I was traveling in the left lane with the speed control set at seventy miles in a seventy-five mile per hour limit area, perfectly awake on a straight part of the road. Suddenly, without any move on my part, the vehicle began to hydroplane. It had been drizzling and the road was a little wet, so I did not want to touch the brakes. Unfortunately, I was not quick enough to disengage the speed control, so the truck kept pushing to keep its seventy-miles-per-hour speed.

All the inertia of this heavy vehicle was heading directly to the far right of the highway, where there was a drop off the side of the road, and there was no way to recover control. I knew I was going to either die right there or end up in the emergency room with a lot of physical injuries. I was approaching the edge of the road, and since there was nothing I could now do, I closed my eyes. I let go of the steering wheel and said, "God in Your hands."

The first blow was incredibly strong, and I could not help but release a scream of fear, while I still kept my eyes closed. The car tumbled and rolled, with terrible noises of destruction all around. My body was shaken in all directions, firmly held by my seat belt. But I dared not open my eyes. I believed the pickup truck was off the road and rolling. I felt that if I opened my eyes, I would not allow God to perform the miracle for me. And yes, I needed a miracle at that moment to come out of this one alive.

After what seemed like a long time but must have been only several seconds, the vehicle came to a stop. I opened my eyes and realized I was still alive. I had no pain, but probably that was because of the high adrenalin. I would start to feel pain any second now, I thought. I checked myself all over to see where the blood and the injuries might be, but I could see no injuries at all. Finally, to my amazement, I understood that I was completely unscathed. It was incredible! Unbelievable!

I looked out the window, only to discover that my car was upright on its four wheels in the middle of the highway, on a ninety-degree angle to the direction of travel. It was late at night, so there was little traffic, but I could see the lights of one vehicle coming towards me in the distance. I had to get out of there. My first instinct was to get out of the car, but then I noticed the engine was still running...another surprise. I put it in reverse and was able to get the Tundra off the road and onto the shoulder. What an incredible product Toyota makes, I thought.

As I am writing these lines, two of the big three automakers in the United States, General Motors, and Chrysler are struggling financially and asking the government for a $50-billion bailout loan. Many of the highly rated quality vehicles are manufactured in the United States by their competition. For decades, these big two companies have lagged behind Toyota and other well-established brands in quality. So no wonder these companies are struggling.

Once parked in a safe zone, I closed my eyes again and took a deep breath, thanking Jesus and Mary for what I felt was another chance. For the second time, my life had been spared. It became immediately clear to me that God had given me a vivid demonstration of what can happen when you place your life in His hands: He can perform miracles. I felt very strongly in my heart that if I had opened my eyes, the reality would have been different. You see, my vehicle was completely destroyed, but I did not even have a scratch. I usually get scratches when I work in my garden or doing some home chores, but after this terrible accident I had no injuries, not even minor ones...absolutely nothing.

As I continued my thinking that night while I waited for help to arrive, it started to become evident that God was telling me to take the bold move: quit now and close my eyes. That as He took care of me in this accident, He would take care of me after I quit my job. I had to leave this job and trust that God would be there for me. I had to trust that things would turn out well. However, doubts haunted me.

If I left, how would we make ends meet financially? How would we pay for the mortgage, the cars, the schools, and the credit cards? Was I ready to step down from a high-powered job, with prestige and recognition? How would this impact me personally later? How would this be perceived by my partners? Would they feel I was abandoning them at a bad time? What about friends and family? Would they look at me funny and think that I am crazy?

All these questions and fears filled my mind, and I had no reassuring answers to them. So I could not bring myself together to quit immediately. This decision would have to wait. I was not following God's direction, despite the fact that He was talking to me loud and clear. That is what is admirable about Mary and Joseph; they are so *obedient*. Despite the craziest requests from God, they just do as He says, with no excuses or delays. Very admirable, I believe.

The road taken by the Holy Family to Egypt was not free of danger. One day they were attacked by robbers, but something stopped the attack. Instead, the Holy Family was escorted to one of the thieves' homes and offered much-needed shelter. The youngest child of this couple had a strange illness that covered his body with a skin rash or irritation. This child was later going to participate in another episode related to Christ. He became one of the thieves that were nailed to the cross next to Jesus. He was the one that asked Jesus to intercede for him before God. Mary told the mother of the child to bathe him in the same bath water where she bathed Jesus. The mother did just that, and the child was cured. This was one of the first miracles of the healing powers of Jesus.[3]

Another interesting episode on the journey to Egypt was when the Holy Family found themselves in the middle of nowhere with no water. Mary and Joseph prayed to God for help, and a spring of water appeared in this place, which exists to this day. This is how, with much help from the above, the Holy Family was able to make and survive this difficult trip to Egypt with a newborn baby.

Eventually, after many days, they arrived in Heliopolis in Egypt.[4] The city was full of decadence, because it was a time when Egypt was not a strong kingdom. People lived there without much hope and had succumbed to sinful lifestyles. As the Holy Family entered the city, several special events took place that made them be feared by the people of this town. The first one happened as they were walking the streets, one of the pillars, or altars, of one of the Egyptian gods collapsed, bringing down the image and completely destroying it. Later, as they walked past a temple, again another image inside the temple collapsed and was destroyed.

The Holy Family had given away to charity most of the treasures given to Jesus by the wise men, but they had kept a small portion, which helped them pay for a residence in Matarea, the place where they finally settled. The place they selected was extremely poor and simple and had no nearby water. Close by was a water well that had dried up many years earlier, but as soon as Mary approached it, the well began circulating water again. This helped the Holy Family enormously, because otherwise they would have had to fetch water from far away. In this way, Mary was able to bathe baby Jesus and give him the proper care.

Joseph's carpentry talents were well received in Egypt, where

---

3 *The Lowly*, I, 297

4 *The Lowly*, I, 301

apparently no other carpenter had the skills to do the type of work he did. So Joseph was able to quickly generate income to sustain the family. The Holy Family stayed in the same house throughout their time in Egypt. They were able to practice their religion freely, and other Jewish families living in the vicinity would join them in these practices.

After four years, Joseph was informed by the angel of God that they could now journey back to Nazareth.[5] Mary and Joseph could not contain their happiness, because they badly wanted to return to their homeland. They quickly packed their bags and started off on their way back. Jesus was four years old now and could walk on his own.

It seems that after the Holy Family returned to Nazareth, things had calmed down. King Herod thought he had killed everyone who could have become the king of the Jews. So their life proceeded normally for the first time in many years. This must have been a real relief for Mary and Joseph after what they had gone through.

Taking into account that Jesus' grandmother Anna came from the line of the Essenes and that the Essenes on Mount Carmel had come from Nazareth, it would not be unexpected that the Essenes ways were taught to Jesus in his early life. Later, many of the practices of the Essenes were taught by Jesus, including the concept of life after death, the need to live simple lives, the need to share your wealth with the poor and not sacrifice animals, to name a few.

By the time Jesus began his ministry at the age of thirty, Joseph had already died, and Mary was living alone. There was no way that Joseph, being an earthly man, could have been able to go through what was to come during Jesus' ministry, so God took him back before all of that would happen. Mary, on the contrary, was built to withstand all the pain, suffering, and humiliation that were to come.

Did Mary Have Other Children?

Mary's Perpetual Virginity was well established in the faith by the second century after Christ. It means that Mary was a virgin before,

5 *The Lowly*, I, 314

during, and after giving birth. Origen (185–254 AD), who was an early Christian scholar and theologian and one of the most distinguished of the early fathers of the Christian church, in his *Commentary on Matthew*, expressly states his belief in Mary's perpetual virginity.

> This Virgin Mother of the Only-begotten of God, is called Mary, worthy of God, immaculate of the immaculate, one of the one. [Origen, Homily 1(244 AD), in ULL, 94]

The position of the Roman Catholic Church is very clear and has never changed in this respect: Mary lived and died as a virgin. This position is supported by the Eastern and Oriental Orthodox Churches. Martin Luther and his contemporaries agreed with the Perpetual Virginity of Mary. However, many liberal Protestants now disagree with this position. Martin Luther said, "In childbirth and after childbirth, as she was a virgin before childbirth, so she remained." The contrary position that states that Mary did have other children is based on the references to the "brothers and sisters" of Jesus mentioned in the New Testament.

> This is the carpenter, surely, the son of Mary, the brother of James and Joset and Jude and Simon? His sisters, too, are they not here with us? [Mark 6:3 NJB]

> This is the carpenter's son, surely? Is not his mother the woman called Mary, and his brothers James and Joseph and Simon and Jude? His sisters, too, are they not all here with us? [Matthew 13:55 NJB]

The other argument for the contrary position, also from the New Testament, states that Jesus was Mary's "firstborn son."

> And knew her not till she had brought forth her firstborn son: and he called his name JESUS. [Matthew 1:25]

The New Testament mentions Jesus' *adelphoi*, which can mean literally either brothers or metaphorically refer to countrymen, people, or believers.[6] The Protoevangelium of James, an Apocryphal Gospel (applied to the books that were considered by the church as useful, but not divinely inspired) probably written about 150 AD, presented these *adelphoi* as Joseph's children from a previous marriage, stating that Joseph married Mary after he had become a widower; that would make these *adelphoi* Jesus' step-brothers.

One of the "brothers" of Jesus is called Joset in Mark 6:3 and Joseph in the corresponding Matthew 13:55. However, since in Judaism children are rarely named after the father, it is unlikely that Jesus' "brothers" were biological children of Joseph. Thus, the Protoevangelium of James is probably incorrect.

In Maria Valtorta's visions, many are related to Jesus' cousins: James, Joseph, Simon, and Jude are the sons of Mary and Alphaeus, the brother of Joseph. So we have two Marys in the story: Mary, the Mother of God, married to Joseph, and the other Mary, married to Alphaeus, the brother of Joseph. James and Jude, or Judas Thaddeus, were disciples of Jesus.

Anne Catherine Emmerich also refers to Jesus' cousins being the sons of Mary Cleophas, who was the wife of Alphaeus. [See Anne Catherine Emmerich's Genealogic Chart in the Appendix II.] Mary of Alphaeus, or Mary Cleophas, is also mentioned in the Gospels of John and Mark as Mary the wife of Clopas. [John 19:25–27, Mark 15:40]

The lack of references to Joseph in the Gospels after Luke 2 would confirm the Emmerich and Valtorta visions that he was dead during Jesus' ministry. It was customary that when a husband died, the wife would join the family of the closest relative, in this case Alphaeus. The children of this family grew up with Jesus and were called his brothers and sisters, since in Aramaic there was no other term for them.

Regarding the reference to Mary's firstborn son, it was a practice since ancient Israelite times to give more importance to the firstborn

---

6 Perpetual virginity of Mary. In Wikipedia. Retrieved August 28, 2008 from http://en.wikipedia.org/wiki/Perpetual_virginity

son. As we read in Chapter 2, Sarah's only son Isaac was also called first born. It should not surprise us then that there would be references to Jesus as the firstborn son, even when Mary had no other sons.

Another point worth mentioning is that Mary was a descendant of the Essenes. As discussed in earlier chapters, it was not uncommon for them to practice celibacy. When She is visited by Angel Gabriel in the Annunciation, Mary says: how can this be, if I am a virgin? With this statement, Mary is saying that although She is already married to Joseph, She is still a virgin. This confirms that Joseph and Mary until then had preserved Mary's virginity.

Later, after the birth of Jesus, comes the story of Salome, who would not believe that Mary's virginity was preserved until she could physically verify this for herself. Salome is taken to Mary, who allows Salome to inspect her body and verify her virginity.

My personal opinion is that it would not make sense for Mary, after having gone through everything She had experienced, to give up Her virginity. Mary wanted to devote her life to God, and for this She pledged to Him Her virginity. She was forced to marry but lucky enough to find Joseph, who agreed to preserve it. After the miraculous events of conception and birth of Jesus, it would make no sense for Her to abandon her virginity.

It also does not make sense for Mary to have had six other children, including James, Joseph, Simon, Jude, and at least two sisters, and then to be entrusted to the disciple John by Jesus when he was dying in the cross. Maybe if these six other children were actually Mary's children, then Matthew and Mark would have referred to them in their writings as the "children of Mary" instead of the "brothers of Jesus."

In any event, it seems that the New Testament scripture could support either position; thus it is up to the reader to reach a conclusion which best resonates with his or her faith.

The Presentation of Jesus in the Temple

In Jewish law, the first-born male had to be consecrated to the Lord, and as such, Mary and Joseph had to present baby Jesus in the Temple in Jerusalem. There is a bit of a confusion between Matthew's Gospel and Luke's Gospel here; Matthew [2:13] tells that the Holy Family had to flee to Egypt right after the visit of the wise men; while Luke [2:22] tells us the Presentation was soon after Jesus was born, therefore before the trip to Egypt.

Anne Catherine Emmerich's version is that the flight to Egypt took place after the Presentation. Joseph's dream took place when he was already back in Nazareth and not in Bethlehem. In any event, Jesus was presented in the Temple in Jerusalem, and it was here that Mary was reminded of the bitter future that awaited Her by the words of old Simeon.

> And, behold, there was a man in Jerusalem, whose name was Simeon; and the same man was just and devout, waiting for the consolation of Israel: and the Holy Ghost was upon him. And it was revealed unto him by the Holy Ghost, that he should not see death, before he had seen the Lord's Christ. And he came by the Spirit into the temple: and when the parents brought in the child Jesus, to do for him after the custom of the law, Then took he him up in his arms, and blessed God, and said,
>
> Lord, now lettest thou thy servant depart in peace,
> according to thy word:
> For mine eyes have seen thy salvation,
> Which thou hast prepared before the face of all people;
> A light to lighten the Gentiles,
> and the glory of thy people Israel.
>
> And Joseph and his mother marvelled at those things which were spoken of him. And Simeon blessed them, and said unto Mary his mother, Behold, this child is set for the fall and rising again of many in Israel; and for a sign which shall be spoken against; (Yea, a sword shall pierce through thy own soul also,) that the thoughts of many hearts may be revealed. [Luke 2:25–35]

What is important to understand from this chapter is the huge sacrifice that Mary undertook in *obedience* to God: being nine months pregnant and still taking a long trip from Nazareth to Bethlehem, shortly after, taking an even longer trip with a newborn baby from Bethlehem to Egypt, then living in Egypt for several years in extreme poverty, when She could have returned and lived in the comfort of Her home in Nazareth. The presentation of the child Jesus was also a demonstration of *obedience* and much humbleness. This was the Son of God, why would She need to present Him to anybody? All this is admirable and shows the virtues of this holy woman called Mary.

Chapter 8

Love of God

Mary's life during Jesus' ministry was very difficult because people did not understand the mission of the Messiah, whereas Mary understood it perfectly and supported her Son all the way. Since the conception of Jesus in her womb, Mary knew what awaited Jesus: that he would provide her many joys, but also be the source of the greatest pains that would pierce her heart.

It must have been difficult to live with the knowledge that your son would die at a young age, that he would be tortured to death. When I look at my children, I cannot imagine this. Even the thought of it makes me turn my mind quickly away from the subject. My mind does not even want to consider the possibility of something like this happening.

We have to understand that Jesus' attitude in His last three years of life, during His ministry, was that of a revolutionary. Jesus stepped over Jewish traditions, both religious and related to family affairs. At the time people were not ready to accept this. This caused Mary great sufferings and humiliations. Her own relatives would not accept Jesus' behavior, and they could not understand how Jesus had basically relinquished his responsibilities for taking care of his mother, one important Jewish tradition.

We will be quoting the writings of Maria Valtorta frequently in this chapter, because they help us understand what was going on in Mary's life at the time, how She felt and dealt with these situations. When I read Maria Valtorta, it is as if I were savoring the best ice cream; each page was like a spoonful of creamy ice cream slowly melting in my mouth. The reading was so delightful that it made my eyes water at times. I feel that in the case of Maria Valtorta, I will offer literal quotes because I don't think that there is any other way to convey the love and the feelings contained in her writings.

Jesus told Maria Valtorta:

> "The Gospels had described Me well enough to save souls, at least. The Blessed Virgin, however, was little known. Her personality was described incompletely; too many things were left in the dark. Now I have revealed Her. I Myself have given you this perfect account of My Mother. She is the Glory of Orderliness...Her name adorns the Orderliness [of all things]..." [*The Virgin Mary in the Writings of Maria Valtorta*. Fr. Gabriel Roschini, page 22-23]

Maria Valtorta does an exceptional job of portraying Mary. Some quotes are quite lengthy, but worth the time. The first one is from Jesus' third year of ministry, in his small humble home in Nazareth. Jesus is speaking to the apostles, the shepherds, and the women disciples about the Annunciation.

> Jesus bends gently over Mary Who has slid to His feet, almost ecstatically, in the recollection of the remote hour, shining with a special light, which seems to issue from Her soul, and He asks Her in a low voice: "Which was Your reply, Most Pure Mother, to him who assured You that by becoming Mother of God, You would not lose Your perfect Virginity?"

And Mary, almost in a dream, slowly, smiling, Her eyes shining with joyful tears: "I am the handmaid of the Lord! Let it be done to Me according to your Word," and She reclines Her head on the knees of Her Son, adoring Him.

Jesus covers Her with His mantle, concealing Her from everybody's eyes and he says: "And it was done. All will be done until the end. Until Her next transfiguration and the one after that. She will always be the 'Handmaid of the God'. She will always act according to what 'the Word' says. My Mother! That is My Mother. And you ought to begin to become fully acquainted with Her holy Figure ... Mother! Mother! Raise Your face, My beloved ... Call Your devout admirers back to the Earth, where we are for the time being ..."

...Mary raises Her face wet with tears and whispers: "Why did You do that to Me, Son? The secrets of the King are sacred..."

"But the King can reveal them whenever He wishes. Mother, I did it, so that the words of the Prophet may be understood: 'A Woman will enclose the Man in Herself' [Jeremiah 31:21–22], and the words of the other Prophet: The 'Virgin will conceive and give birth to a Son.'" [Isaiah 7:14] [*The Poem*, III, 404–405]

Note the reference made by Jesus to "Her next transfiguration and the one after that." The next transfiguration, I presume, would be the virginal conception of Jesus, and the following one would be Mary's Assumption in body and soul. Another splendid description is given by Jesus when he talks to Simon in his first year:

"There is a Flower there [in Nazareth]! There is a Flower that lives solitary, fragrant with purity and love for Her God and Her Son! There is My Mother. You will meet Her, Simon, and then you will be able to tell Me whether there is a creature like Her, also in human Grace, on the earth. She is beautiful, but everything is surpassed by what emanates internally from Her. If a brute should divest Her of all Her clothes, should disfigure Her and send Her roving, She would still appear as a Queen in royal dress, because Her holiness would cover Her as a mantle and confer splendor of Her. The world can give Me all possible evil, but I will forgive the world everything, because to come into the world and redeem it, I had Her, the humble and great Queen of the world, Whom the world does not know, but through Whom it has received God and will receive still more throughout centuries....

... I solemnly tell you that the true House of God, the Holy Ark, is Her Heart, the veil of which is Her most pure flesh and its embroidery work are all Her virtues." [*The Poem*, I, 455-456]

We have to understand that before and during Jesus' ministry, women in Israel and Judah were considered below man, secondary and not worthy. Women could not eat at the same table as men. Many times in the Old and New Testament we find references to this. The women always ate at another table, separate from men. So it was Jesus' goal to elevate the stature of women. He starts with His own mother but continues throughout His ministry to give women the preponderance they deserved.

In one conversation recorded by Maria Valtorta, the Scribes become scandalized when another woman starts praising Mary. Jesus has to intervene and correct them:

The scribes say: "She's mad! She's mad! Make her keep quiet. She's either mad or possessed. Order the spirit possessing her to go away."

"I cannot. There is no spirit in her but God's, and God does not eject Himself."

"You are not doing it because she praises You and Your Mother and that tickles Your pride."

"Scribe, meditate on what you know about Me and you will see that I know no pride."

"And yet only a demon can speak in her to sing the praises of a woman thus!... A woman! And what is woman in Israel and for Israel? What, but sin in the eyes of God? The seduced and seducer! If it were not part of our faith, one could hardly believe that woman has a soul. She is forbidden to go close to the Holy [of Holies] because

> of her uncleanliness. And this woman says that God descended into Her!... " says another scandalized scribe and his accomplices aid and abet him.
>
> Jesus says, without looking at anybody in the face. He seems to be speaking to Himself: "The Woman will crush the head of the serpent". [Genesis 3:15]
>
> "The Virgin will conceive, and give birth to a Son Who will be called Immanuel..." [Isaiah 7:14] "A shoot will spring from the stock of Jesse, a flower will come up from this root and the Spirit of the Lord will rest on Him." [Isaiah 11:12] "That Woman. My Mother. Scribe, out of respect for your knowledge, remember and understand the words of the Book."
>
> The Scribes do not know what to reply. They have read those words thousand of times and said that they were true. Can they now deny it? They keep quiet. [*The Poem*, IV, 703]

Because of the secondary nature of women in the culture of the time, it should not surprise us to find during the centuries that followed that Mary would play a secondary role in the nascent Church. Although she has been adored by many saints, the inspiration of many writers throughout the centuries, and in the hearts of the devout Christians since the beginning of times, the Church throughout its history has had at best a lukewarm attitude towards Mary.

Even today when you go to most Catholic Church masses in the United States, there is no reference at all to Mary, except one mention of Her name in the Creed prayer. Some churches may include Her name in the Penitential Rite as well. There is no mention in the readings, none in the sermons, and certainly none in the rest of the liturgy of the mass. In Latin America, you will find a greater acknowledgement of Mary; at the end of the mass some priests pray the Hail Mary. The devotion with which Mary is celebrated will vary from church to church and will depend greatly on the priest who officiates the mass.

The tradition, the popular sentiment, transferred between generations has kept Mary alive. Mostly grandmothers and mothers have maintained the tradition. Were it not for this, Mary would have all but disappeared from active Christian faith. Few men have been active followers of Mary.

Saint Louis Marie Grignion De Montfort, who lived between 1673 and 1716, was one of these men. He wrote what is considered one of the best works on Mary, his *True Devotion to Mary*. He not only brought Mary to the front line but also clearly explained how we can more easily reach God when we go to Him through Mary.

Saint Louis de Montfort says in his wonderful book that God Himself, being such a perfect being, had to lower Himself in order to come to us humans, who are still so far from perfection. To do this He chose to come to us through Mary, His own creation.

Mary was the *bridge* which God took to close the huge gap between His magnificence and our pettiness. In the same way, when we want to reach God through His son Jesus, we should go through Mary. She can embellish, purify, and present our petitions and devotions to Jesus in a more untarnished way, in a way that is more pleasing to the Father.

Saint Louis de Montfort gives us an excellent example. Suppose you are a peasant who wants to honor his king. You go to the court with an apple that you want to give to the king. You quickly realize that you are not dressed in the most presentable way, and probably you are not well versed in how to address the king. So you opt to give the apple to the queen, in the hope that she will find a better way to present it to the king.

The queen takes your apple; she polishes it and makes it very shiny. She then places this apple on a golden tray and goes to present it to the king. The king marvels at this beautiful gift of yours, and he sends you all his blessings. Saint Louis de Montfort says that this is the way in which Mary acts in our behalf before Jesus.

We humans cannot even see how tarnished our souls are, and, says Saint Louis de Montfort, we believe that we can go directly to God and He will hear us. Nothing could be further from the truth, he says; we are so far from God that we need to go to Him through Mary. God created this channel for Him to come down to us and for us to go up to Him. Mary can best teach us how to love God, because She carried Him in Her womb and cared for Him for thirty-three years.

Love of God

A most important requirement in this path of enlightenment is loving God. Mary in Her life showed us what love for God really is and how we should make this our everyday task. In a resent message from the visionaries in Medjugorje, Mary said:

> Mary's Message of April 25, 2008, from Medjugorje: "Dear children! Also today, I call all of you to *grow in God's love* as a flower which feels the warm rays of spring. In this way, also you, little children, grow *in God's love and carry it to all those who are far from God.* Seek God's will and *do good to those whom God has put on your way*, and be light and joy. Thank you for having responded to my call." [www.medjugorje.net]

This is not new. Mary has said this in Her messages innumerable times. Jesus also said it many times throughout His public life. The clearest mention of the love of God is probably recorded in His first commandment:

> And thou shalt love the Lord thy God with all thy heart, and with all thy soul, and with all thy mind, and with all thy strength: this is the first commandment. [Mark 12:30]

Can we really love someone we don't really know? Can we love someone who is far, a distant stranger? To be able to love God, we have to know Him personally. God sent us Mary first, and through Her, He sent us Jesus, so we would know Him. Through the example of these two very special human beings, we can know who God is. This entity, whom no one knows directly, is best represented by Mary and Jesus. In Them we have a vivid picture of who the Lord God is. If you can love Mary or Jesus, you can love God. If you get to know Mary and Jesus intimately, you will love God even more. How do you reach enlightenment, then? You love Mary and Jesus with all your heart, with all your soul, with all your mind, and with all your strength.

> Mary's Message of January 25, 2006, from Medjugorje: "Dear children! Also today I call you to be carriers of the Gospel in your families. Do not forget, little children, to *read Sacred Scripture*. Put it in a visible place and witness with your life that you believe and live the Word of God. I am close to you with my love and *intercede before my Son for each of you*. Thank you for having responded to my call." [www.medjugorje.org]

There isn't much to read about Mary in the Bible, so it is difficult to get to know Her this way. I suggest you read the works of Maria Valtorta and Anne Catherine Emmerich referenced in this book to really get a feel of who this splendid woman was. I can confidently say that these readings were a turning point in my life. They showed me more about love than what I could have ever imagined. They changed my life.

In no way am I suggesting you should not read sacred scripture; quite the contrary. I believe you should also read the Bible as often as you can, ideally every day. Sacred scripture and the writings of these two incredible visionaries complement each other very well. In reading both of their works, you will learn more about Jesus as well.

> Mary's Message of October 25, 2007, from Medjugorje: "Dear children! God sent me among you out of *love* that I may lead you towards the way of salvation. Many of you opened your hearts and accepted my messages, but many have become lost on this way and have never come to *know the God of love with the fullness of heart*. Therefore, I call you to be *love and light* where there is darkness and sin. I am with you and bless you all. Thank you for having responded to my call." [www.medjugorje.org]

With the message above, Mary is asking us for true conversion of heart. She speaks about the superficial conversions of people who "do not walk the talk." These people have perhaps discovered only part of the truth: the story of Mary and Jesus. But they have not discovered the most important part, which is the love that They represent. The love that They want us to embody every day, every minute of our lives.

> Judge not, that ye be not judged. For with what judgment ye judge, ye shall be judged: and with what measure ye mete, it shall be measured to you again. And why beholdest thou the mote that is in thy brother's eye, but considerest not the beam that is in thine own eye? Or how wilt thou say to thy brother, Let me pull out the mote out of thine eye; and, behold, a beam is in thine own eye? Thou hypocrite, first cast out the beam out of thine own eye; and then shalt thou see clearly to cast out the mote out of thy brother's eye. [Matthew 7:1–5]

We must seek God's will in our lives, we must be charitable and not judge; we must pray fervently; we must meditate in silence. But most of all, we must *love God with the fullness of our hearts.* In doing this we will be able to forget the "I am" and learn that we are nothing without Him that made us. We should be prudent not to trust our actions if they are void of God's love.

> <u>To Mirjana Dragicevic-Soldo on March 18, 2007:</u> "Dear children! I come to you as a Mother with gifts. *I come with love and mercy.* Dear children, mine is a big heart. In it, I desire all of your hearts, purified by fasting and prayer. I desire that, *through love, our hearts may triumph together.* I desire that through that triumph you may see the real Truth, the real Way and the real Life. I desire that you may see my Son. Thank you." [www.medjugorje.net]

As a man, as an engineer, and as a businessperson, it has not been easy for me to fully open up to Mary. I had some initial reservations, because in a way it seemed as a sign of weakness. What would my friends say? Was I wimping out? But slowly and surely Mary conquered my heart. I must also say that I was very fortunate to have the support and encouragement of my wife. I don't know if I would have been equally successful if she was not supporting me all the way. It has to be difficult to move ahead in your spiritual development if your partner is not on the same page.

In the end, it is about courage, about wanting to awaken to God so badly that you do not care about the consequences. Why should I care what people say about me if the one who really matters is God? I am conscious that I am walking the road less traveled, but I also realize that this is the only way for me to reach enlightenment. I know today that some of my close relatives are concerned about the contents of this book, that I may step on the toes of their beliefs and cause them embarrassment with their friends. If I allowed myself to be concerned about this, my book would never have been written. Should I live by what others expect of me? Or should I live by what my heart tells me?

Balancing out my values and personal beliefs with my job in the "real world" has not been simple either. Many times I have been faced with very difficult decisions that have put me to the test, like God put Abraham to the test. Much to the dissatisfaction of some of my colleagues, I sometimes had to take the decision that my heart was calling for. In many situations when I was not clear, I would say that I had to think about the issue before making a decision. This allowed me to bounce it in my heart for a while; invariably the decision came. It always helped to think what Jesus would have done if He were in my shoes at that moment.

Making business decisions in an inspired way does not mean you will not make difficult decisions, or that you will tolerate mediocrity, or that you will always yield to the other parties' point of view. Jesus himself taught that we need to be strict and tough with people who are not doing things properly. Remember that Jesus stomped in the Temple in Jerusalem and kicked out the merchants who had transformed the Temple into a marketplace.

My more difficult decisions always had to do with asking a nonperforming subordinate to leave the company. The usual process I would follow was to give honest feedback to an employee early in the assignment and continuously thereafter. If this did not help, then the next step was to try to find a better match for this person's talents in another job in the company. If this still did not work, then the next step was for me talk with the person directly and explain the situation. I would usually say what I truly believed in my heart: that there was another excellent job waiting for this person outside the company; a much better match for the excellent talents he or she had.

Other difficult decisions had to do with client's demands, who usually wanted to get their services for less than what we believed they were worth. Sales would sell beyond our capabilities; Operations would say we could not do it with the existing resources; Finance would say we would lose money if we took on this project. Where was the right answer? Balancing out the need for gaining new clients that led to growth with short-term financial goals was always a struggle for me. But in the end, I always managed to make decisions that had the consensus of most people and required a bit of compromise from all.

In these situations I would always bring people together by describing the vision of the company in two or three years and what getting there entailed. The vision included a collection of topnotch clients that would generate the revenues required and that would be willing to work with us in a partnership, not in a traditional client-vendor relationship. It also included offering a creative and innovative service on our part that was not available in the marketplace. This often required something new, and my recommendation to my co-workers was to meditate in silence and find the inspiration to come up with the answers.

Other times, the decisions had to do with mistakes on our part that the client did not necessarily know about, when some of our people wanted the client to assume the cost. These were the easy decisions for me. If we made a mistake, we had to assume our full responsibility. We had to go to clients and explain the situation, letting them know that we would fix it at our cost, even at the expense of our bottom-line profits. If we had a good partnership with the client, this approach always worked. With other less tight client relationships, it sometimes cost us the client. For me the means never justified the end result.

It was not uncommon for me to pray silently in my office for guidance, to call upon Mary to clear my mind and give me the inspiration I needed at that time. Then who better than Mary, the Daughter of God, to be our advocate in front of God when we elevate our prayers through Her? In Maria Valtorta's writings, Mary is called the Father's Daughter, the Son's Mother, and the Holy Spirit's Spouse.

Sometimes before a difficult meeting, or in the middle of one, I would silently pray and ask for Mary's divine help. Most of the time, situations would resolve themselves favorably; but other times they would not. In such situations I would not lose my temper, and instead I thought that this was a better resolution, that God knew something I did not and was directing the events so that in the end things would work out for the better. It was this trust in God that allowed me to stay serene and in control, even in the most difficult situations.

When I think about my difficulties and the ones that Mary had to endure, I realize how insignificant my life has been compared to Her life. Think only of how Mary must have suffered for thirty-three years, knowing that Her son was to be tortured and die in the cruelest way. What woman can withstand this pain? We know from experience that the greatest sorrow a woman can experience is the death of a son or daughter.

Many times after the death of a son or daughter, the mother has consequences that may last for the rest of her lifetime. Some such consequences are deeply rooted psychologically, so that the person is never the same again. Maybe in this context it is easier to understand how Mary lived with this knowledge. This is why it is said that Mary's heart was also pierced.

During Jesus' ministry, in His Mother's house in Nazareth with Mary of Alpheus, Mary's sister-in-law, present, Jesus made a reference to His imminent death:

"Jesus!" shouts Mary of Alpheus, springing to her feet, frightened, looking around as if she were afraid to see deicides appear from behind hedges and trunks of tress. "Jesus!" she repeats, looking at Him painfully.

"What? Do you perhaps not know the Scriptures since you are so surprised at what I say?" asks Jesus.

"But...But...It is not possible...You must not allow that...Your Mother..."

"She is Savior like Me, and She knows. Look at Her. And imitate Her."

Mary is in fact austere, regal in Her deep pallor. She is motionless, with Her hands in Her lap clasped as if in prayer. Her head is straight, looking into space...

Mary of Alpheus looks at her. She then addresses Jesus again: "All the same, You must not mention that horrible future! You are piercing Her heart with a sword."

"That sword has been in Her heart for thirty-two years."

"No! It's not possible! Mary...always so serene...Mary..."

"Ask Her, if you don't believe what I say."

"I will ask Her! Is it true, Mary? You know?"

And Mary in a gentle but firm voice says: "It is true. He was forty days old and I was told by a holy man [Simeon]...But also previously...Oh! When the Angel told Me that while remaining the Virgin, I would conceive a Son, Who would be called the Son of God and is such because of His divine conception, when I was told that, and that in the barren womb of Elizabeth a fruit had been formed [John the Baptist] by a miracle of the Eternal Father, I had no difficulty in remembering the words of Isaiah: 'The Virgin will give birth to a son and they will call Him the Immanuel' [7:14] ... All, all Isaiah! And where he speaks of the Precursor...And where he speaks of the Man of sorrows, stained with blood, unrecognizable... a leper...for our sins...The sword has been in My heart since then and everything has served to drive it in more deeply: the song of the angels and the words of Simeon words and the visit of the Kings from the East, and everything..." [*The Poem*, IV, 126]

Jesus love for His Mother was huge, and He had no problems showing everyone how much He loved Her. Maria Valtorta's writings are full of beautiful descriptions of this. Mary usually, in her humility, becomes embarrassed with Jesus' comments. When asked by one of the Apostles why His favorite flower was the lily of the valley, Jesus responded:

> "This is my reply: 'Because of its humility.' Everything in it speaks of humility ...The spots it loves...the attitude of the flower...It makes Me think of My Mother...This flower...so tiny! And yet how sweet is the perfume of one flower alone. The air around it is scented by it...My Mother also...humble, reserved, unknown, She asked only to remain unknown...And yet the perfume of Her holiness was so strong that it drew Me from Heaven..." [*The Poem*, III, 802]

When Jesus begins his ministry and leaves home, it is a most difficult moment for Mary:

> Jesus is speaking to Mary. At first I do not understand the words which are just whispered, and Mary nods Her head in assent. Then I hear: "And get Your relatives to come. Don't stay here alone. I will be happier, Mother, and You know how I need peace of mind to fulfill My mission. You will not lack My love. I will come quite often, and I will inform You in case I cannot come home when I am back in Galilee. Then You will come to Me, Mother. This hour was to come. It began when the Angel appeared to You; it is now striking, and we must live it, Mother, must we not? After we have overcome the trial, we shall have peace and joy..."
>
> ...Jesus and Mary stand up and they look up to Heaven: two living victims shining in the darkness...
>
> ...Jesus takes His dark blue mantle, puts it on His shoulders, and pulls the hood on to His head. He arranges His haversack across His back, in order to be free when walking. Mary helps Him, and She delays endlessly in sorting His tunic, mantle and hood, caressing Him in the meantime.
>
> Jesus goes towards the door, after making a sign of blessing in

> the room. Mary follows Him, and at the open door they kiss each other once again.
>
> The road is silent and solitary, white in the moonlight. Jesus starts walking away. He turns round twice to look at His Mother, Who is leaning against the doorpost, paler that the moon's rays, Her eyes sparkling with silent tears. Jesus moves farther and farther away along the narrow white road. Mary is still weeping against the doorpost. Then Jesus disappears round a bend of the road.
>
> His Evangelical journey, which will end on Golgotha, has just begun. Mary goes into the house shedding tears and closes the door. She also has started Her journey, which will take Her to Golgotha. And for us... [*The Poem*, I, 236-238]

The relationship between Mary and Jesus was very loving and special, particularly in face of what Mary already knew. She knew He was the son of God, and She knew She would not have Him for too long a time, that He would be sacrificed for the salvation of mankind. All these notions could not but enhance the love She felt for Her Son and for all of us. Mary was willing to give up Her Son for you and me!

Chapter 9

Suffering and Disobedience

Once Jesus starts His ministry, troubles begin for Mary because Her relatives would not understand or accept the work of Jesus. They were particularly harsh with Jesus and Mary for this reason. Imagine the situation: Here you are, living your life the best you can under a government that was not tolerant of dissent, in a religious order that did not welcome new ideas or changes to the status quo. Then imagine your nephew is speaking truths that upset the established religious order. This nephew could get himself killed or put you and your whole family in great danger.

Furthermore, Mary was quite lonely after Jesus left. Should Jesus die, there would be no one to take care of her, so some relatives would have to assume that responsibility. Her parents had died, and Joseph had died some years earlier. The only person who was there for Her and from whom She would receive love was Jesus. Here are comments of Jesus on this subject:

> "...Mary, a gentle woman, with perfect love, (because in the Virgin Full of Grace also affections and sensations were perfect), also Mary had but one good thing, and one love on the earth: Her Son. The only thing left to Her. Her parents had died a long time

> before. Joseph had died some years earlier. Only I was left to Her to make Her feel She was not alone. Her relatives, because of Me, of whose divine origin they were not aware, were somewhat hostile to Her, because they considered Her a mother incapable of imposing Herself on Her Son, Who did not behave according to good common sense, and turned down marriage proposals which could bring prestige to the family, as well as material help.
>
> Her relatives reasoned according to common sense, to human sense—you call it good sense, but it is only human sense, that is selfishness—and they would have liked My life to comply with their usage. After all, they were always afraid that one day they might get into trouble because of Me, as I had already dared express certain ideas which they considered too idealistic and thought they might irritate the Synagogue. Hebrew history was full of teachings on the fate of Prophets. The Prophet's mission was not an easy one, and often brought about death for the prophet and trouble for his kinsfolk. And there was always the fear that one day they might have to take care of My Mother.
>
> They were, therefore irritated by the fact that She did not oppose Me in anything, nay, She seemed to be in perpetual adoration in front of Her Son. This conflict was to increase in the three years of My public life, when it culminated with open reproaches every time they met Me in the midst of crowds and were ashamed of what they considered My mania for vexing the powerful classes. And they rebuked Me and My poor Mother!" [*The Poem*, I, 239]

Continuing with the example of your hypothetical nephew: if he started speaking about those painful realities that we all turn our heads from; if he started upsetting the established religious order to which you have grown accustomed, then surely you would resent him. That is the reality of "the road less traveled." People who are not content with the established order and who have the courage to disagree publicly are frowned upon. We do not want others to remind us of what is wrong in our lives. That is exactly what Jesus was doing, with the full support of Mary and the corresponding painful consequences for Her.

This brings to my mind the business environment, where most people are so quick and eager to please others, for the sake of professional advancement or to protect their jobs. People who seem to be very close to God, who preach about the need to follow Christ, are victims of their own ambitions and fears. When the going gets difficult, God suddenly becomes a second priority, and earthly, ego-based needs take precedence. It is the sad reality of our lives.

In another well-known story, when Jesus is a guest at a wedding in the city of Cana, Mary asks Jesus to use his powers and provide wine for the party. It was very embarrassing for the hosts of the party to run out of wine, so Mary requested this miracle from Her son. Jesus initially rejected the petition because His time to go public had not yet come. However, he yielded to Mary's request and turned water into wine for the benefit of all those in the party, who marvel. Here is a conversation between Jesus and his cousin Jude Thaddeus, upon inviting him to the wedding.

> "I wanted to tell You...Jesus...be careful...You have a Mother... She has but You...You want to be a 'rabbi,' different from the others, and You know, better than I do, that...that the powerful classes do not allow anything which may differ from the customary laws they have laid down. I know Your way of thinking...it is a holy one...But the world is not holy...and it oppresses saints...Jesus...You know that fate of Your cousin the Baptist...
>
> ...You...what are You going to do? To what fate are You going to expose Yourself?" [*The Poem*, I, 277]

We are all drawn in opposite directions by the needs of the world and the need to please God. Unfortunately, we place our needs ahead of God's, because we either are not comfortable with a path of uncertainty or because of fear. The reality is that when we do this, we are mortgaging our souls; we are borrowing from God's eternal fountain of grace. We fail to realize that we will have to pay this mortgage back, and in this case, there will be no government bailout.

Mary understood this clearly. She knew that Jesus' mission was of God and not of the Earth, and as such She supported Her son all the way. Mary was the only one who, according to Jewish law, could reprimand Her son, but She never did. On the contrary, She was always there for Jesus and never asked anything of Him, except His love. Ever since Mary had Jesus, She knew She would lose Him, but She never allowed Her human needs to be above those of God. The only perfectly obedient human being aside from Jesus was Mary.

Mary knew that during the most difficult times of His upcoming passion, everybody would abandon Him except Her. She would always be there for Him. If it were up to Her, She would gladly die with Her Jesus and sacrifice Herself. Mary's love and devotion to God and to Jesus was complete. This loving attitude drew me to Mary. Little by little, Mary was conquering my own heart with Her uncompromising purity, love, and obedience. The tough, former macho man, who practiced martial arts and played rugby when he was younger, was being won over by the most gentle, tender, pure, and loving soul of Mary.

It should not be hard for us to understand then the love that Jesus had for His Mother. Just as Mary had only Jesus to pour Her motherly love over, Jesus only had Mary as the recipient of his most pure feelings of love. Here is a vivid description of Jesus' love for His Mother. Upon returning to Nazareth in His first year, He tells Her:

> "...Oh! Mother! How I miss You!"
>
> "Tell Me to come, Son, and I will..."
>
> "...Oh! My Joy, tell Me what you lacked. Your servant, My Lord, will endeavor to provide."
>
> "Nothing, but You..."
>
> "...Let Me look at You, to My hearts' content, holy Mother of Mine..."
>
> "...I have come with My disciples and friends. But I left them in Melcha's wood. They will come tomorrow at dawn. I...I could not wait any longer. My Mother!..." and He kisses Her hands. [*The Poem*, I, 475]

As Jesus' ministry proceeds and as He begins to antagonize the established religious ways, His job becomes more difficult and His persecution begins. Jesus feels the pain of the rejection of mankind, just like you and I feel the rejection of people when we say things that do not please them. Mary tries to alleviate Jesus' pains of rejection with Her motherly love. However, in doing this, Mary has to keep to Herself Her own pains.

Jesus mentions also the necessity of approaching women to redeem them and His grief at not being able to do so owing to the wickedness of men.

> Mary nods assent and then She decides: "Son, You must not deny Me what I want. From now on I will come with You when You go away. I will come at any time, in any season, to any place. I will defend You from false accusations. My simple presence will cause the mud to fall off. And Mary [of Alpheus] will come with Me. She is so anxious to. That is what is needed near the Holy One, against the demons and against the world: a mother's heart." [*The Poem*, II, 36]

Mary does indeed accompany Jesus on some of His travels, and He presented Her as "the Apostle." This is very relevant to our time, because today Mary does not occupy this privileged role beside Jesus. I wish I could one day see an image of Jesus holding hands with Mary, just walking besides each other like two normal human beings.

Here is what Jesus told an elderly couple when He presented His Mother:

> "...Is that Your Mother?" asks the landlord.
>
> "Yes, She is. I brought Her here to you, because She also is not in the group of My disciples. The last to be received, the first in faithfulness. She is the Apostle. She preached Me even before I was born...Mother, come." [*The Poem*, I, 572]

When Jesus says "the last to be received," I believe He is referring to our times. Mary is the last one to be received. She is being received now in many places in the world, through Her apparitions and the many conversions taking place in the world because of Her. She is also being received by you as you read this book, and hopefully She will find a permanent place in your heart, just as She found in mine.

With Mary joining Jesus, other women begin to also follow Jesus. In Cana, Susannah, the bride at the wedding, joins Jesus. In Beth-Tsur, a woman called Eliza begins to follow Jesus. Back in Nazareth, Mary of Magdala joins Mary, who brings her to Capernaun to meet Jesus. At this point Martha, Lazarus' sister, also joins them. Mary and the group of women traveled with Jesus through many towns and joined Him in His mission to spread the good news.

It is important to note here that Jesus treated women as equals. He gave them a rightful place next to Him. The women stayed with Jesus in His most difficult times, when all the disciples, except John, had run away. Therefore, it is only fair that Mary and the women should have been given a proper place in the Christian church. However, not just Mary but all women were left on the sidelines by the men who started it all.

When Jesus and the women went through towns where Mary of Magdala had previously caused scandals, Jesus' enemies, took advantage of the opportunity to criticize Him. This caused Mary great pain:

> "...I feel as if My heart were wrapped in burning thorns. And every time I breathe I am pierced by them. But He must not know! I strive to appear serene, in order to support Him by My serenity. If His Mother does not console Him, where is My Jesus going to find comfort?" [*The Poem*, II, 546]

When they all go to Jerusalem, Mary is distressed to hear of the traps that have been set up for Jesus. She knows that the danger is high, but She still wants to be close to Her Jesus. Mary weeps and Jesus says to Her:

> "...It is for the love of men. Let us drink our chalice with good will. Is that right?"
>
> Mary stifles Her tears and replies: "Yes." A tortured heart-rending "yes." [*The Poem*, III, 41]

In Jesus' third year of ministry, as the time of the passion comes closer, during a stay in Nazareth, Mary of Alpheus has a conversation with Mary about Jesus' upcoming death. They are talking about the sword been driven into Mary's heart.

> [Mary of Alpheus asks.] "And You are so calm? So serene? Always the same as when You arrived here, a young bride, thirty-three years ago, and I remember it so well that it seems yesterday to me...But how can You?...I...I would be mad...I would do...I don't know what I would do...I...No! It is not possible for a mother to know that and be calm!"
>
> "Before being a Mother I am daughter and servant of God... Where do I find my tranquility? In doing the will of God. From where does my serenity come? From doing that will. If I had to do the will of a man, I might be upset, because a man, even the wisest can always impose a wrong will. But the will of God! If He wanted Me to be the Mother of His Christ, have I perhaps to think that that is cruel, and in that thought lose My serenity? I am to be upset by the thought of what Redemption will be to Him and to Me, [yes] also to Me, and how I will be able to overcome that hour?" [*The Poem*, IV, 127]

Doing God's will is not always going to be easy. It was not in Mary's case, knowing that the future held Jesus' death and Her suffering. Understanding Mary's situation was so important for me. She found the serenity and peace of mind She needed in Her difficult situation by trusting God. Her example inspired me to be able to take the steps that were required in my personal life—to trust God over everything else and truly believe that despite the appearances, His recommended course of action was the better one.

> [Later on, Mary said:] "I am the Mother of everybody...and I must not be the Mother of one only. I am not even the Mother of Jesus exclusively...You see how I let Him go away without holding Him back?...I would like to be with Him, that is true. But He deems that I should stay here until He will say: 'Come'. And I am staying. His days of rest here? My joys of a mother. My peregrinations with Him? My joys of a disciple. My solitude here? My joys of a believer who does the will of Her Lord." [*The Poem*, IV, 147–148]

Understanding Mary's role as the Mother of all helped me receive Her as my Mother and allowed me to start a conversation with Her that has not stopped to this day. In Her I have found the serenity I needed. In Her I have felt peace of mind, knowing that I am doing God's will, even though the circumstances may not be favorable.

As the time of Jesus' passion draws closer, both Mary and Jesus start preparing for the inevitable event. Jesus gave the following words to Maria Valtorta, addressing all of us:

> "When you think about Mary, I would like you all to meditate on Her agony. It lasted thirty-three years and climaxed at the foot of the cross. She went through that for you. For you, the crowd laughed at Her, thinking that She was the mother of a madman. For you, the relatives and people of distinction made reproaches to Her. For you, I seemed to disavow Her when I said: 'My Mother and brethren are those who do God's will.' However, no one outdid Her in doing God's will, a formidable Will that imposed on Her the torment of watching Her Son being tortured. For you, She wore Herself out, meeting Me here and there. For you, Her sacrifices: beginning with leaving Her home to mingle with the crowds, going as far as leaving Her native land for the hustle and bustle of Jerusalem. For you, She put up with [Judas], who was brooding treason in his heart. For you,

> She grieved when I was accused of being a heretic or possessed by the devil. Yes, all that for you. You do not realize how much I loved My Mother... I grieved when I saw My Mother suffering, when I had to lead Her to Her torment like a harmless ewe, and when I had to put Her through so many farewells: the one when I left Nazareth to evangelize; the one I showed you in a vision and which took place before My imminent Passion; the one before the Last Supper when My Passion was already on its way with Judas Iscariot's betrayal; and the atrocious farewell on Calvary." [*The Virgin Mary in the Writings of Maria Valtorta*. Fr. Gabriel Roschini, page 152]

Five days before His death, Jesus went to say goodbye to His good friend Lazarus. Jesus is very concerned about His Mother and Her health as She faces the inevitable. This is what He told Lazarus:

> "My Mother!...Oh! How heart-rending it is to speak of Her!... Mother is already so distressed! She is also dying exhausted...She also has been dying for thirty-three years, and She is now one big sore, like the victim of an atrocious torture. I swear to you that there has been a struggle between my mind and My heart, between love and reason, whether it was right to send Her away, to send Her back to Her house...
>
> ...But I cannot, no, I cannot do that. Poor Jesus, laden with the sins of the world needs consolation. And Mother will give Me it. And the even poorer world needs two victims. Because man sinned with woman; and the Woman must redeem, as the Man redeems...
>
> ...She has wept through-out Her life of a Mother. She no longer weeps now. She has crucified Her smile on Her face...Have you noticed what Her face has become these last days? She crucified Her smile on Her face to comfort Me. I ask you to imitate My Mother." [*The Poem*, V, 375–376]

The next day, the Wednesday before Passover, Mary finds Jesus sleeping in the grass, and she sits close to Him. When Jesus wakes up, they talk about the impact of *disobedience on mankind*:

> "Mother, when You are all alone, who will You stay with?"
>
> "With whomsoever You will tell me, Son. I obeyed You, Son before having You. I will continue doing so after You have left Me." Her voice trembles, but a heroic smile is on Her lips.
>
> "You know how to obey. How restful it is to be with You! Because, see, Mother? The world cannot understand, but I find complete rest with obedient people...Yes. God rests with the obedient. God would not have had to suffer, to toil, if disobedience had not come to the world. Everything happened because man did not obey. That is why there is sorrow in the world...That is the reason for Our grief." [*The Poem*, V, 453–454]

Notice what Jesus is saying: There is *suffering* in the world because of *disobedience.* If we obeyed God's will, then we would not suffer. Men and women in all corners of the world are trying to find a way out of suffering. Buddha, around 500 to 400 BC, discovered that the cessation of suffering leads to self-awakening and enlightenment. He went on to describe the "Noble Eightfold Path," which is a technique that leads to the cessation of suffering. It involves or requires the right view, right intention, right speech, right action, right livelihood, right effort, right mindfulness, and right concentration. Are we not talking about the same thing here?

> For as by one man's disobedience many were made sinners, so by the obedience of one shall many be made righteous. [Romans 5:19]

> And this is love, that we walk after his commandments. This is the commandment, That, as ye have heard from the beginning, ye should walk in it.. [2 John 1:6]

I mentioned earlier in the book that I had *disobeyed* God many times, but the clearest case was when I felt a call from God to leave my job and did not do it. I had not been able to come to terms with myself and make the decision right there and then. I thought about it long and hard, but the best I could do was to come to the decision to leave in June 2008, a full seven months after my car accident on November 30, 2007—certainly not the type of response God wanted from me.

In December, the company started having problems with our English partners and experienced the first month of financial loss after a sustained period of profits. Our partners wanted to gain control of the company; of course, we, the founding partners, did not want to give up control. There is something special in the business world about having control. It gives the owners of that control a sense of power that feeds egos and provides a false sense of security.

The pressure from England grew stronger by the day, reaching a point in January where top level conversations had practically halted. One of the company's major global clients was defaulting on its payments, and the company was facing a cash flow squeeze. Taking advantage of this, England was delaying its payments to us for services provided. Although the company could continue making its payments, day-to-day management of the company was very difficult.

At the time, we were trying to get an agreement with England that would give them the control they wanted in exchange for reasonable and fair cash compensation. I was not keen on hanging on to power, since I had already decided to step down in a few months. But I did want to make sure that the agreement we would reach would be fair for all parties. Unfortunately, the subject of fairness is not usually the same for all parties involved in a dispute. Each party has its own personal views on the subject, and they are usually quite different. Thus, we could not come to an agreement.

In late February, no agreement was yet in sight. On a positive note, our major client had resumed payments. We had lowered our cash consideration for relinquishing control far below what we felt was reasonable and fair, but England was not budging. The next step was to bring in the lawyers and take our disputes to court. I was distressed that the people who had been our partners, and to some extent our friends, could behave this way.

We had expanded this company many-fold over the past years and had secured some lucrative global clients. Our name was becoming well-known and respected in the industry. Our only fault was that we did not want to give up control of the company for less than its fair value. We did not deserve this treatment, I thought.

On Wednesday, February 27th, another shareholder meeting that did not take us anywhere had just broken up. My frustration was increasing by the hour. I could fight competition with all my strength, but to also have to fight our partners at the same time was too much. I was starting to feel the stress of the last three months in my body, something I did not welcome. My skin was showing signs of irritation that I could not really trace to anything else but stress. Being a cancer survivor, I knew how bad this can be for your health.

I went into the conference room and locked myself in there for a while. I wanted to meditate and decide on my next steps. I began my usual routine with breathing exercises and prayers. I asked Jesus to hold my left hand and Mary to hold my right hand, and I asked them for direction. What should I do next? Should I continue this battle for control? Should I accept the offer made by England, although this would make me highly unpopular with my U.S. partners? What should I do?

As had become usual for me in these circumstances of need, the answer came back quickly. I felt enveloped by a strong energy that made my heart vibrate at a very fast pace, and the answer came as clear as water. "Place your resignation now!" I suddenly realized that the last three months of hardship in the company and in my life had occurred because I had not heeded God's command back in November. He had given me a second chance in my life under the condition that I would leave my job immediately. I did not listen and thought that I could make things happen in a better, more orderly fashion if I worked all the details out before leaving. Well, I was wrong.

I finished my meditation and immediately wrote my resignation letter and sent it to the Board of Directors of the company. I packed my things and left the office. No one saw me leaving since it was around lunch time, and most people were either out to lunch or in the cafeteria. I walked Lincoln Road down to the beach, walked Ocean Drive all the way to my hotel, immersed in my thoughts. Then I grabbed a bathing suit and went swimming in the ocean along beautiful Miami Beach. I felt at peace with myself; I had finally been able to gather the courage to jump into the void.

I now look back and realize that I brought this situation upon myself. While it was easy to blame my partners in England, the struggle was the best thing that could have happened to me. I have no grudges against them. In fact, I respect them highly for their accomplishments and hope that some day we will be able to embrace again. With regards to my domestic partners, I hope they may fully understand that they too brought this upon themselves in some way. But most importantly, I hope that they may forgive me for jumping ship ahead of time.

On the Thursday before Passover, just before the Last Supper, Jesus went again to Mary to say goodbye to His Mother. In this episode, we see Jesus' human side and his need for motherly comfort. He is about to undergo a painful Passion and knows that everyone will turn their backs on Him. Mary, the loving Mother, is there for Him, and instead of breaking down because of Her own pain, she finds the strength to comfort Jesus.

> "Mother, I have come to get strength and comfort from You. I am like a little baby, Mother, who needs the heart of his mother for his grief, and his mother's breasts for his strength. In this hour I have become Your little Jesus of a long time ago. I am not the Master, Mother. I am only Your Son, as in Nazareth when I was a little boy, as in Nazareth before departing from My private life. I have but You. Men, at the present moment are not friendly with and loyal to Your Jesus. They are not even brave in doing good. Only the wicked are constant in doing evil. But You are faithful to Me and You are My

strength, Mother, in this hour. Support Me with Your love and Your prayer." [*The Poem*, V, 490-491]

After instituting the Eucharist in the Last Supper and distributing it to His Apostles, Jesus took a piece of the consecrated Bread and the chalice of consecrated Wine to His Mother, who was in another room, to give Her communion. He then returned to the Apostles.

It is so hard to grasp the above episode and understand the serenity with which Mary accepted the whole situation. Any other mother would have grabbed her son and not let him go. Any other mother would have broken down in major pain. But Mary knew that if She externalized Her feelings, She would make the situation even harder for Jesus.

Mary submitted Herself in total obedience to the will of God. Just as She had earlier said "Let it be" when the angel announced She would conceive the son of God, She had to let Her son go. As in the song "Let it Be," She let her Son be, according to the will of God. This is the perfect obedience of Mary and Jesus that redeemed us and undid the Fall. Eve's sin was undone by Mary, as Adam's sin was undone by Jesus. Both Mary and Jesus, through their perfect obedience and suffering, saved all of us.

This magnificent, incomprehensible sacrifice, only fully understood by God Himself, gave humanity a second chance; a chance to live again in the likeness of God; a chance to become what Adam and Eve were before original sin. A simple act of *disobedience* created suffering for mankind, the reality we have always been living.

Christ's death did not change that for all of us immediately; albeit many souls have been saved by Christ's sacrifice. Only when we recognize the full sacrifice of Redemption from both Jesus and Mary will we be capable, by the pure grace of God, of benefiting from the full extent of the Redemptive sacrifice of them both. Only then will the reality of a new Earth become available for us and provide us with the gifts that were originally given to humans in Adam and Eve. It is the birthright of all, because Mary and Jesus came for all people of all creeds and faiths.

Let us then embrace Mary in Her full capacity. Let us embrace Mary and Jesus together, because that was God's original intention. Since the beginning of time, the Word, the Eternal Thought of God, encompassed Mary and Jesus. Let us recognize this important reality, and let us become the image and likeness of God. This was God's original intent and is what we are called to become.

Mary is here, installed on Earth now, so we may become aware of Her, so we may get to know Her, so people like you and me, curious enough about Her appearances, will investigate the source of these events. In Her wisest way, with Her usual humbleness, Mary has been here for decades, patiently waiting for me and others to write about Her, and for you to read about Her. This is the Time of Mary, the Age of Mary, or the Day of Mary, as it has been called by others. Are you ready for Her?

Chapter 10

The Way Back to Paradise

We all know how Jesus died after the terrible torment He was subjected to, Mary had to find Herself and cope with the situation. Her Son was dead. All Her life She had been devoted to Jesus, according to the will of God. What now? God had not made this clear to Her. Just as Jesus felt abandoned by God in the final hours on the cross, Mary also felt God's abandonment, except that Her torment was longer, as She waited for Jesus' resurrection.

Hours followed of terrible angst, with the Apostles and disciples still in great fear because they had not yet seen Jesus, and the Holy Spirit had not yet descended upon them. Most of them did not believe that Jesus would resurrect. John the Apostle was entrusted to take care of Mary, and He began to do so. But he wasn't the consolation that Mary needed, because nothing could replace Jesus; Her Jesus, so close to Her heart and now gone. How difficult those days must have been for Mary.

Mary knew Jesus was going to resurrect after three days, because He had said so, but the pain was still too great. She could not take any nourishment. She was slowly dying of pain while She waited for the resurrection of Her son. When Jesus' dead body was being prepared in the sepulcher, Mary had tremendous trouble letting go.

> "O soul of My Jesus, o soul of My Christ, o soul of My Lord, where are You? O cruel hyenas joined to Satan, why have you taken away the soul of My Son? And why have you not crucified Me with Him? Were you afraid of committing a second crime? (Her voice is becoming stronger and stronger and more and more heart-rending). And what was it for you killing a poor woman, since you did not hesitate to kill God Incarnate? Have you not committed a second crime? And is letting a mother outlive her murdered son not the most nefarious crime?..."
>
> ...She straightens Herself up again and says to those present in a loud voice: "Go away, all of you. I will stay. Close Me in here with Him. I will wait for Him. What are you saying? That it is not possible? Why is it not possible? If I had died, would I not be here, lying beside Him, waiting to be put in order? I will be beside Him, but on My knees..." [*The Poem*, V, 631]

Mary was finally convinced that She must let go of Jesus' body and was pulled away by Mary Magdalene. The preparation of Jesus' body was completed by two other people, and the stone was placed in front of the sepulcher. Jesus spoke the following words to Maria Valtorta:

> "And the torture continued with periodic attacks until dawn on Sunday. In My Passion I had only one temptation. But the Mother, the Woman, expiated on behalf of women, guilty, several times, of every evil. And Satan behaved mercilessly with infinite cruelty towards the conqueress.
>
> Mary had defeated him. The most atrocious temptation for Mary. Temptation against the flesh of the Mother. Temptation against the heart of the Mother. Temptation against the spirit of the Mother. The world thinks that Redemption ended with My last breath. No it did not. The Mother completed it by adding Her treble torture to redeem the treble concupiscence, struggling for three days

> against Satan, who wanted to induce Her to deny My word and not to believe in My Resurrection. *Mary was the only one who continued to believe.* She is great and also blessed because of that faith." [*The Poem*, V, 637-638]

After the sepulcher was closed, Mary ran back to the stone and tried to open it with Her hands, but it was too big and heavy and She could not. She continued to try to move the stone and wept, repeating her request to be left there alone: She would wait for Her Son for three days, and She would see Him resurrected. At this point, Mary Magdalene talked to Her and convinced Her to leave and go with them. She appealed to Mary's duty as Mother of all and the need of those around them for comfort, faith, and Motherly love.

> It is the Magdalene who finds a reason capable of bending the Sorrowful Mother to obedience. "You are good, You are holy, and You believe, and You are strong. But what are we?...You are aware of it! The majority have run away. Those who have remained are trembling. The doubt, which is already in us, would overwhelm us. You are the Mother. You have not only duties and rights on Your Son, but also duties and rights for what belongs to Your Son. You must come back with us, among us, to gather us together, to reassure us, to infuse Your faith into us..."
>
> "...You are right. I must go back...and look for the apostles...the disciples...the relatives...everybody...And say...say: have faith. Say: He forgives you...Who have I already told so?...Ah! The Iscariot... I will have to...yes, I have to look also for him...because he is the biggest sinner..." Mary remains with Her head bent on Her breast, trembling as if She were disgusted, and then She says: "John, you will look for him. And you will bring him to Me. You must do that. And I must do that. Father, let also this be done for the redemption of Mankind. Let us go." [*The Poem*, V, 641]

Maria Valtorta describes in detail the great pain that Mary was subjected to. Mary never condemned God for what had happened. Most mothers would have had an argument with God and perhaps even distanced themselves from God. But not Mary. She stoically remained loyal to Him, despite the difficulties, the pain, and the sorrow. Here are some excerpts that describe how Mary was feeling:

> "How many! How many wounds! How much sorrow! Oh! My Jesus, My Jesus so wounded! So wounded! So wounded! No. No. Lord, no! It cannot be true! I am mad! Jesus dead? I am raving. Jesus cannot die! Yes, He can suffer. But He cannot die. He is the Life! He is the Son of God. He is God. God does not die." [*The Poem*, V, 655]

> "Simeon said so: 'And a sword will pierce Your heart.' A sword? A mass of swords! How many wounds did they inflict on You, Son? How many groans did You utter? From how many spasms did You suffer? How many drops of blood did You shed? Well, each of them is a sword in Me. I am a mass of swords. There is not a strip of skin on You without sores. In Me there is not one that has not been pierced. They pierce My flesh and penetrate My heart." [*The Poem*, V, 656]

> Then Jesus tells Maria Valtorta: "...And She did not curse, She did not hate. She prayed, She loved, She obeyed. Always a Mother, to the extent of thinking, among Her tortures, that Her Jesus needed Her virginal veil on His innocent body, to defend His decency, She was able to be at the same time the Daughter of the Father of Heaven and obey His dreadful will in that hour. She did not curse, She did not rebel. Either against God, or against men. She forgave the latter." [*The Poem*, V, 670]

Most incredibly, Mary was the only one who kept the faith in Jesus' resurrection, while all others were doubtful or didn't believe.

> Mary speaking again to Mary of Alpheus: "Mary, I am fond of you and you are relative of Mine. Later, you will tell your sons, the apostles, so that they may persevere in their apostolate and tri-

> umph over Satan. I am sure that, if I had accepted the doubt, if I had yielded to Satan's temptation and I had said: 'It is not possible for Him to rise from the dead' denying God—because to say that was the same as denying God with His Truth and Power—such a great Redemption would have come to nothing. I, the new Eve, would have bitten once again at the forbidden fruit of pride and of spiritual sense, and I would have destroyed the work of My Redeemer..."
> [*The Poem*, V, 682]

I do not know how you feel about all this, but when I discovered the incredible suffering of Mary, I could not but admire Her more. It became increasingly difficult for me to understand how this incredible woman could be ignored and forgotten. I had to do something about it. I had to contribute in my way and bring Mary back to life.

The last passage about faith reminds me of my car accident and the moment in which I closed my eyes and put my life in the hands of God. I am certain, completely certain, that if I had opened my eyes the outcome of the accident would have been different. I would have been either dead or severely injured. Mary persevered, despite the doubts of everyone else. I kept the faith and trusted in a positive resolution for my accident, and it turned out well. We have to keep faith and trust in God over all things.

After two days, on Sunday morning, Jesus appeared to Mary Magdalene, who had gone back to the sepulcher. [John 20:1–18] She was filled with joy and ran to tell Mary and the Apostles. Jesus, in a separate comment to Maria Valtorta, explains that He rose from the dead ahead of the three-day period because of the needy prayers of His Mother.

> Jesus says: "The fervent prayers of Mary have anticipated My Resurrection by some time.
>
> I had said: 'The Son of man is about to be killed, but on the third day He will rise from the dead.' I died at three o'clock in the afternoon of Friday. Whether you count the days by their names, or

> you count them by their hours, they were only thirty-eight instead of seventy-two, in which My Body had remained lifeless. With regards to the days, it should have been the evening of the third day to say that I had been in the sepulcher three days.
>
> But Mary anticipated the miracle. As when with Her prayers She opened the Heavens a few years in advance of the predetermined time, to give the world its Salvation, so now She obtains some hours in advance to give comfort to Her dying heart." [*The Poem*, V, 712]

Then the resurrected Jesus appeared to two disciples who were walking to Emmaus, a town about seven miles from Jerusalem, and he walked along with them. [Luke 24:13–35] He talked to them about the scriptures and about the role of Jesus, who had to die to save mankind. Eventually they arrived at Emmaus, and they invited Jesus to stay with them because it was already late. While at dinner, while breaking bread, the disciples finally recognize Jesus, and He disappears. "Did not our heart burn within us, while he talked with us by the way, and while he opened to us the scriptures?" [Luke 24:32] They then immediately return to Jerusalem to tell the others.

Mary, the disciples, and the Apostles were reunited and discussed these apparitions of Jesus, which confirmed that He had resurrected. Mary had already assumed Her role as Mother of all, and She was feeling a little better because She knew Her son had resurrected. She was able to give comfort to the Apostles and to the men and women disciples who had not yet seen Jesus and who still did not fully believe. Mary's strength is admirable.

Then Jesus made His most glorious appearance to Mary and all the Apostles except Thomas. [John 20:19–23] He appeared to them, perfectly recognizable. He even had wounds on His hands and feet. All the Apostles and Mary marveled at the event. This was the final demonstration of the Redemption of mankind.

Eight days later, Jesus appeared again to the Apostles. During this appearance, Thomas the Apostle must stick his finger into Jesus' wounds to believe that He was actually there with them. Jesus told Thomas, "Thomas, because thou hast seen me, thou hast believed: blessed are they that have not seen, and yet have believed." [John 20:29]

This passage has always impressed me. I feel Thomas' experience serves as a testimony for all of us. How many of us do not believe if we do not see for ourselves? I have to thank Thomas, because in his nonbelief, he had Jesus demonstrate—for him and for a lot of us—His resurrection.

The meaning of Jesus' resurrection is very significant. He demonstrates that there is life after death. This is the first time that this truth is clearly established for mankind. Although some people of the Jewish faith did believe in life after death before the time of Jesus, until then, it had not been a certainty.

We know the Egyptian Pharaohs believed in life after death through the discoveries in their majestic tombs, but it was not clear to me where most of the Israelites stood on this issue at the time of Jesus. I could find only two references, and they were fairly close to Jesus' time [2 Mac 7:29 and 2 Mac 12:43] in the year 150 BC. In the Old Testament, God promised the Israelites that He would protect them and their future generations from their enemies, if they remained loyal to Him and the Covenant. God did not promise life after death.

We also know from Josephus and Philo, the two ancient historians referenced in Chapter Three, that the Essenes believed in the concept of life after death. We know that the Essenes were the most spiritual group of Israelites, who thrived around the year 150 BC in places like Qumran and Mount Carmel, when the events of Maccabees took place. So it is quite possible that this belief had permeated to other highly devout Jewish people.

In any event, a visible demonstration of life after death had not taken place before Jesus. He was the first human being to demonstrate this for all of us. Interestingly, as we shall see later on, Mary was the second human being able to resurrect in a visible way, thereby also demonstrating life after death. Mary did not make Herself visible right after Her death, but She has been seen and experienced, usually in different ways, for the last two hundred and fifty years. During the recent decades, Mary has appeared much more frequently than during all previous history, and the significance of this cannot be underestimated.

The only explanation that I have for Mary's active participation in the affairs of our time is that the redemption of mankind is not yet complete. Since Jesus' death, close to two thousand years have elapsed; we only have to look around to understand that we still have a long way to go. Jesus, conceived in the immaculate womb of Mary, through His sacrifice opened the gates of Heaven for us, which had remained closed since the Fall of Adam and Eve.

> And no man hath ascended up to heaven, but he that came down from heaven, even the Son of man which is in heaven. [John 3:13]

> And, behold, the veil of the temple was rent in twain from the top to the bottom; and the earth did quake, and the rocks rent; And the graves were opened; and many bodies of the saints which slept arose, And came out of the graves after his resurrection, and went into the holy city, and appeared unto many. [Matthew 27:51–53]

Could it be possible that God has allowed these two thousand years to elapse so mankind could progress spiritually—to prepare us for the completion of our redemption process? Could it be possible that we are in the critical period of mankind's redemption right now? Sometimes it looks like that to me. On the few times I tune into the television news or read the newspaper, I get the impression that the world is enduring complicated times on all fronts. We are facing forces we cannot control, like hurricanes, earthquakes, flooding, and global warming.

Mankind has been able to overcome most of the afflictions that Mother Nature has thrown our way over the past two thousand years. But I am not sure this will be the case in the future. In March 2008, I was in the Chilean Patagonia with Beatriz, and we could experience directly the effects of global warming on the glaciers, which are receding and melting down. Miles of rock and land formation that a few years ago were covered with ice are now dry, and the marks of the erosion process of millions of years is totally visible; sad evidence of the huge effects that humans have brought upon Earth.

Until I started writing this book, my selfish position was that it is very likely there will be natural disasters in the future and that many lives will be lost because of that, but I really was not feeling all that sorry for the people that could lose their lives. Of course, I thought that my family and I would be spared disaster, that somehow we would manage not to be at the wrong place at the wrong time when disaster hit.

I regret to say that I am not alone in this position. I have heard similar thoughts expressed by other people, who believe that the world cannot sustain six billion people or more. The notion is that a "cleansing" has to take place to give the Earth a chance to recover and sustain itself in a more balanced way, without the stress created by the needs of so many people.

Mary's message is different. She says we can all be saved: "God desires to convert the entire world" [June 25, 2007]; "I want to save you and, through you, to save the whole world." [July 30, 1987] Her message is about raising the awareness of all humankind, because we cannot continue to live our lives in the way we do today. We need to make some changes, and if we make these changes, we can become what God envisioned for us to become: the light beings of His creation.

We can become the new Adams and new Eves. When we attain this status, the issue of natural resources is no longer relevant. The issues of global warming and disasters are no longer relevant. These issues are left behind on the old Earth and are no longer part of our reality. The new Earth can be closer to where it once was—Paradise. Anne Catherine Emmerich in her visions saw Paradise. She said that Paradise exists right now, except that we cannot see it. We do not have access to it. At least this was the case in the late seventeen hundreds.

> Paradise is still in existence, but it is utterly impossible for man to reach it. I have seen that it still exists in all its splendor. It is high above the earth and in an oblique direction from it… [*The Lowly*, I, page 6]

Jesus, talking to Maria Valtorta, also reinforced the concept of Him and Mary overcoming the Fall of Adam and Eve. This is an important concept that we must try to fully comprehend. Although it is symbolic, it is also extremely relevant. In New Age language, or in Oriental terminology, we could refer to the Fall as the "karma of mankind," which was erased by the Passion of Christ and Mary.

In Chapter 1, the major sin during the Fall was described as Adam and Eve's *disobedience* to God. Now we understand that human Redemption was obtained by Jesus and Mary through their perfect *obedience* to God. Jesus and Mary erased the negative karma brought upon mankind by Adam and Eve.

> Jesus said to Maria Valtorta: "The couple Jesus-Mary is the antithesis of the couple Adam-Eve. It is the one destined to cancel all the behaviour of Adam and Eve and take Humanity back to the point in which it was when it was created: rich in grace and in all the gifts granted to it by the Creator. Humanity has undergone a complete regeneration through the deeds of the couple Jesus-Mary, who have thus become the new Founders of the Human Family. All the previous time has been cancelled. The time and story of man are reckoned as from this moment in which the new Eve, through a complete change and inversion of creation, and through the deed of the Lord, from Her immaculate womb generates the new Adam.
>
> But in order to cancel the behaviour of the two First Parents, the cause of deadly illness, of perpetual mutilation, of impoverishment, even more: of spiritual indigence—because after their sin Adam and Eve found themselves completely despoiled of everything, and it was infinite wealth, the Holy Father had given them—these two Second Ones had to act in everything in a manner completely opposed to the way of dealing of the two First Parents. So they had to carry their obedience as far as the perfection that lowers itself and sacrifices itself in its flesh, feelings, thoughts and will, in order to accept everything that God wants. So they had to carry their purity to the degree of absolute chastity, whereby the flesh...what was the flesh to Us two pure ones?" [*The Poem*, V, 582]

When I think of what perfect obedience to God means to me in my life, I do not associate it with chastity or with a level of perfect purity. Not at this stage of my life, at least. However, I do associate it with using my free will to express my love to God, to my neighbors, and to Mother Nature. Every time I give thanks to God for a beautiful day or for something that impressed me in nature, I am expressing my love to God. When I smile at someone in the street, or I help a stranger, I am expressing my love to God. If I do what is right instead of what is more convenient or what I want, I am expressing my love to God.

It is in the simple daily things that we can express our love to God, until we reach a stage of permanent gratitude and constant union with God. You may think, 'This guy is conveniently taking what is useful to him and forgetting the rest.' You may well be right, but you have to start somewhere. I have committed many sins in my life, some terrible ones indeed, but I must have done some things right in my last eleven years, because my life has been filled with ever-increasing blessings. Matthew says:

> Ye shall know them by their fruits. Do men gather grapes of thorns, or figs of thistles? [Matthew 7:16]

I am currently in the best place I have ever been in my life, feeling a deep sense of peace and gratitude. Therefore, I believe God is at peace with me and supporting me all the way. Otherwise the miracles that are taking place on a weekly basis in my life would not be happening. At times in my life I have been "stuck," like a leaf floating in an eddy between rocks in a river. But now I am flowing freely down the river, escaping most of the rocks and eddies along the way. It is, let me tell you, a most wonderful feeling.

> Mary says: "...Oh! The joy of removing from God's heart the bitterness of Eve's disobedience!...
>
> ...I redeemed that sin by going up the same stages as they

descended. Disobedience was the beginning of the downfall: 'Do not eat and do not touch of that tree,' said God. [Genesis 2:17] And man and woman did not respect that prohibition, although as kings of creation they were allowed to touch and eat of everything except of that tree because God wanted them to be inferior only to angels.

The tree: the means to test their obedience. What does obedience to God's commands imply? It implies all possible good, because God commands nothing but good. What is disobedience? It is evil, because it brings about a rebellious mental state in which Satan can be active." [*The Poem*, I, 86]

When Beatriz came into my life, I felt that what I had been praying for over several years had been delivered on a silver platter. My request was not a simple one. I wanted a woman, already with children, who would be very smart, with a huge loving heart for God and humanity, who was pretty and attractive, bilingual in English and Spanish, who liked sports, among other things. I went as far as specifying that I wanted her to be a good skier, because I love skiing and snowboarding but hate not being able to ski with my partner. Very specific, don't you think?

Well, God delivered all of this and more. Not only could Beatriz ski well, but she could follow me across open terrain on my snowboarding adventures. She was not afraid of deep snow and steep slopes. But most importantly, God brought into my life a person full of virtues, who has been an excellent example for me. The fruits that have sprung out of this relationship have been good. "God commands nothing but good," says Mary in the passage above, and that has been the case with us. We have both grown tremendously in our faith and have had so many wonderful experiences that it would take an entire new book to narrate them all.

"I went along the road of the two sinners, but in the opposite direction: I obeyed. I obeyed in every way. God inspired Me to be a virgin. I obeyed. When I loved virginity that made Me as pure as the first woman before she met Satan, God asked Me to get mar-

> ried. I obeyed, elevating marriage to the degree of purity intended by God when He created the First Parents. I was then convinced that My destiny was solitude in marriage and people's contempt because of My holy sterility, when God asked Me to be a Mother. I obeyed. I believed that it was possible and that the word came from God, because I was filled with peace when I heard it. I did not think: 'I deserved it.' I did not say: 'Now the world will admire Me, because I am like God, creating the flesh of God.' No, I did not. I lowered Myself in My humility...
>
> ...Eve wanted pleasure, triumph, freedom. I accepted sorrow, humiliation, slavery. I gave up my peaceful life, the esteem of My spouse, My own freedom. I kept nothing for Myself..." [*The Poem*, I, 87]

During the Passion, Jesus and Mary endured two different types of sufferings. Jesus' suffering was physical: the torture of His body. Mary's suffering was emotional: the torture of Her heart. Both sufferings are equally meaningful for mankind. We know this from our own experience. They are quite different, but both can be equally devastating in our lives. Jesus gave up His Body and His Blood for our salvation. The torture of the heart was Mary's Passion. She gave up Her Heart for our salvation.

The redemptive efforts of Jesus and Mary, then, not only allowed us access to Heaven upon death but also allowed us to progress spiritually. God's timing is different from our timing. His years are measured in centuries. God knew the human race was not prepared to become His glorious creation immediately after the death of Jesus. He knew it would take about two thousand years of our time for us to awaken to the unlimited possibilities of our species.

God knew that progress and technology would turn us away from Him, that they would make us believe that we didn't need God, that through our technological advances we would believe ourselves to be gods and masters of our planet. He also knew that further progress would tilt the balance back to Him. As men discovered the secrets of the minute subatomic particles, the infinitesimal world, along with the discoveries of the infinite, expansive universe, men would come back to understand the role of God and the role of man in the equation of life. Through the combination of scientific discoveries and progress in many modalities of personal spiritual development, man would again become fertile ground for the next step in His redemption work.

God must have decided that the most effective way to complete the redemption of mankind was to send Mary to us. Mary's universal appeal as mother—kind and sweet, non-political—makes Her a perfect messenger for people of all religions and races. Faith, hope, justice, strength, and charity come from Her. Mary is our Advocate in front of God. She will plead our cause to Jesus and obtain for us the favors we request.

> "Oh! The kiss of My Mother! Who can resist that kiss? And then, with Her slender, but lovingly irresistible fingers, She takes My wrist and forces Me to bless. I cannot reject My Mother, but must go to Her, and make Her your Advocate.
>
> She is My Queen, before being yours, and Her love for you makes such allowances that no one can possibly imagine or understand. And even without any word, but only with Her tears, and the memory of My Cross, the sign of which She makes Me trace in the air, She pleads your cause and exhorts Me: 'You are the Saviour. Therefore save.'" [*The Poem*, I, 178–179]

Like St. Louis de Montfort said in *True Devotion to Mary*, the best way to reach the Father is through Mary, and the best way for the Father to reach us is through Mary. She is apt and ready to serve each one of us if we only let Her into our heart's desires. Jesus explains this concept to Maria Valtorta through the episode of the wedding at Cana. He responded the way He did to the disciples so that the world could know that He will grant requests that come to Him through the Mother.

> "When I said to the disciples: 'Let us go and make My Mother happy,' I had given the sentence a deeper meaning than it seemed. I did not mean the happiness of seeing Me, but the joy of being the initiatress of My miraculous activity and the first benefactress of mankind.
>
> Always remember that. My first miracle happened because of Mary. The very first one. It is a symbol that Mary is the key to miracles. I never refuse My Mother anything and because of Her prayer I bring forward also the time of grace. I know My Mother, the second in goodness after God. I know that to grant you a grace is to make Her happy, because She is All Love. That is why I said, Knowing Her: 'Let us go and make Her happy.'
>
> Besides, I wanted to make Her power known to the world, together with Mine..." [*The Poem*, I, 284]

Jesus offered His first miracle because Mary asked Him. He may also do our miracles, provided they are in our best interest, if we bring our requests to Him through Mary. This is the beginning of Mary's new role as Mother of all.

After these many apparitions, Jesus ascends to Heaven, and Mary and the Apostles prepare themselves for Pentecost, when the Holy Spirit is to descend upon them. [Acts 2:1–13] Maria Valtorta explains that after the passing of several years, John the Apostle, who had been entrusted with the care of Mary, told Peter that Mary would take Her body with Her to Heaven upon death. Peter questions John as to how he knew this, and John answers that the Holy Spirit in Pentecost had revealed this to him.

The Assumption

The day arrived for Mary's Assumption, which means that upon death, Mary ascended to heaven in body and soul. The Catholic Church celebrates the feast of the Assumption on August 15th. Maria

Valtorta's description of this event, with its only witness the apostle John, is short but sweet.

John saw the Mother in an unusual state, putting all things in order in Her room and looking at the relics she had keep of Jesus and His Passion. He asked Her why She was doing this, and Mary responded that Her time had come to ascend to Her Son and for John to prepare to be alone. John started crying, with much pain in his heart, because Mary meant more than his own mother to him.

> Mary says: "...But why are you weeping, John?"
>
> "Because the storm of sorrow is stirring up in me. I know that I am about to lose You. How shall I be able to live without You? I feel my heart being torn to pieces at this thought! I shall not be able to stand this grief." [*The Poem*, V, 929]

John helped Mary to Her bed, and shortly after, Her life breath was gone. When John was able to overcome the first waterfall of tears and sorrow, he remembered what the Holy Spirit had revealed to him. He ran out into the garden to gather some flowers and ran back into the room, because he did not want to miss anything. He arranged the flowers around Mary's body and began to talk to Her, as if She were still alive. He told Her he would stay next to Her bed and watch over Her, waiting for the miracle.

> "Now let us put this lamp closer. So, near Your bed, that it may watch over You and keep me company while I watch You, while awaiting for at least one of the miracles that I am expecting and for whose fulfillment I pray." [*The Poem*, V, 933]

John's faith in Mary's Assumption was complete. He did not do what is customary with a dead person. He did not call the others so the proper rites of death could be performed. He just sat there, watching over the dead body of Mary. But after many hours, perhaps a couple of days, he succumbed to sleep.

Then, all of a sudden, a strong light filled the room, a silvery light, shaded with blue, becoming more bright, more intense, making the light of the lamp and the dawn vanish. The same light that had appeared during the nativity of Jesus in the cave in Bethlehem entered through an opening in the roof. Then, engulfed in this monumental light, angelic creatures appeared, accompanied by a harmonious murmuring sound[1].

The angelic creatures placed themselves around the bed; they bent over and lifted the immobile body of Mary. They flapped their wings more vigorously, more loudly, and John began to awaken; in his deep sleep, he had not yet seen anything. At dawn, the angelic creatures, flapping their wings, carried Mary's body up through the opening in the roof, and John finally woke.

He looked at the bed and did not see the body. He then looked up, and he saw the opening in the roof and the body of Mary being carried up by the angelic creatures. He ran outside to watch the miraculous event. He saw the lifeless body of Mary ascend higher and higher, supported by the angels. Then the wind blew some of the flowers that he had placed in Mary's mantle down on to him.

John continued to watch and realized that God had granted him another miracle, because he could now see the event as if he were ascending next to Mary. He saw the Most Holy Mother being received by Her Most Holy Son, who, with indescribable beauty, descended rapidly from Heaven to receive His Mother. He pressed Her to His heart, and together they returned to where He came from. John's vision finished. He lowered his head and thanked God for the joy of contemplating the miracle.

> He says: "Thanks, my God! Thanks! I foresaw that this would happen. And I wanted to be awake, in order not to lose any episode of Her Assumption. But I had not slept for three days now! Sleep, tiredness, joined to sorrow, overcame and defeated me just when Her Assumption was imminent...But perhaps You wanted me to see what, without a miracle of Yours, I could not have seen. You

1 *The Poem.* v, 934

> have granted me to see Her again, although already so far, already glorified and glorious, as if She were close to me. And to see Jesus again! Oh! Most happy, unhoped for and not be hoped for vision!" [*The Poem*, V, 936]

After this, John collected the petals and became aware that his sorrow was no longer there. He knew that he could go into the world to preach and pray the life of Jesus and Mary. With his personal, first-hand knowledge of Mary's life and Assumption, he planned to let the entire world know what had just happened.

On November 1, 1950, Pope Pius XII declared: "By the authority of our Lord Jesus Christ, of the Blessed Apostles Peter and Paul, and by our own authority, we pronounce, declare, and define it to be a divinely revealed dogma: that the Immaculate Mother of God, the ever Virgin Mary, having completed the course of her earthly life, was assumed body and soul into heavenly glory."

Pope John Paul II quoted John 14:3 from the Bible as a scriptural basis for understanding the dogma of the Assumption of Mary, where Christ, in his Last Supper discourses, explained, "When I go and prepare a place for you, I will come again and will take you to myself, that where I am, there you may be also."[2]

Mary is later cited in Revelation, the last mention of Her in the Bible. This reference is the basis of the last glorious mystery, "The Coronation of Mary," in the rosary prayer.

> And there appeared a great wonder in heaven; a woman clothed with the sun, and the moon under her feet, and upon her head a crown of twelve stars: [Rev. 12:1]

This completes the life of Mary during her time two thousand years ago. In the next chapter, we shall look into the life of Mary

---

2 Assumption of Mary. In Wikipedia. Retrieved September 21, 2008, from http://en.wikipedia.org/wiki/Assumption_of_Mary

during the last two hundred and fifty years, with particular emphasis on the last thirty years. Mary's conception, birth, life, and death are all miraculous. Nothing about Mary is common. It is quite surprising, my dear reader, that we know so little about this great woman. Perhaps you agree with me; the common person does not know the Mother at all. We thought we knew Her from the small pieces of information fed to us by the Church or by our families, but we really do not know nearly enough.

With Her life and Passion, Mary completely undid the Fall of Eve in Paradise, just as Jesus undid the Fall of Adam in Paradise. They both redeemed us from our first parents' original sin. Jesus opened the doors of Heaven for us, and Mary is the bridge to help us get there, so we can find eternal life. They showed us the way to the perfection of God. Admittedly, most of us do not follow this way and can only glance at the perfection of God from a distance. Jesus in flesh suffered the pains of humanity. Mary in her heart suffered the pains of humanity. Both sufferings are huge and redemptive. Both sufferings deserve our highest respect and adoration.

Chapter 11

Mary's Resurrection and Messages

Mother Mary has resurrected and is present in the world today in a very active way. Her resurrection is as meaningful as that of Jesus. She is looking for us everywhere and giving us Her loving messages for us to meditate and contemplate upon. Mary is asking us to return to God, to use prayer and fasting as tools that will help us get back home, and She is telling us that there is not much time left.

Mary appears primarily to children and people living very simple lives. There is a hidden message in these choices. Mary has not appeared to people in power positions or to wealthy people. She has not appeared to people in important positions in the Church or in the political establishment. It is as if with Her choices, She is showing us that we must be like children and lead simple lives. Jesus also said that we have to be like children to enter the kingdom of God.

Mary's messages over the years are repetitive, almost unoriginal, when you read a lot of them. Why is this? I believe because She is asking us to do very simple things, in essence. So She has to repeat the same message over and over. We humans have a difficult time with simplicity, with simple messages. Simple in this case doesn't mean unimportant.

> Mary's Message of July 30, 1987, from Medjugorje: "Dear children, this is the reason for my presence among you for such a long time: to lead you on the path of Jesus. I want to save you and, through you, to save the whole world. Many people now live without faith; some don't even want to hear about Jesus, but they still want peace and satisfaction! Children, here is the reason why I need your prayer: prayer is the only way to save the human race." [www.medjugorje.net]

There is some controversy about whether we should believe in apparitions or not. Some very faithful people disregard apparitions all together, because they only believe in the word of the Gospel. But there is evidence in the Bible, as well as from the Church, that confirms the value of believing in credible ones.

There are many references to apparitions in the Bible: for example, when Abraham saw and spoke to three angels of God; when Lot was visited by two angels of God in Sodom; when Jacob wrestled with an angel of God; when Mary was visited by Archangel Gabriel, when St. Paul had a vision that blinded him for three days on his way to Damascus; just to name a few. Many of the prophets and patriarchs had frequent communications with God. Consider the passage of the Transfiguration, where Jesus becomes a light being and is joined by the enlightened presences of Moses and Elijah, who had left the earthly plane many centuries earlier:

> And after six days Jesus taketh Peter, James, and John his brother, and bringeth them up into an high mountain apart, And was transfigured before them: and his face did shine as the sun, and his raiment was white as the light. And, behold, there appeared unto them Moses and Elias talking with him. Then answered Peter, and said unto Jesus, Lord, it is good for us to be here: if thou wilt, let us make here three tabernacles; one for thee, and one for Moses, and one for Elias. [Matthew 17: 1–4]

The Church takes a very conservative, prudent approach regarding these apparitions. It will sanction apparitions only after careful investigation proves them to be authentic, and the process usually takes many years. Even then, its approval of an apparition is usually in the form of acknowledging that there is a source of divine inspiration in the message; that the message does not conflict with the teachings of the Gospel; and that the apparitions bear good fruits. The Church will also leave it up to the faithful to believe or not in the apparitions. Fr. René Laurentin, one of the world's foremost Mariologists and investigator of Marian apparitions, says the following:

> Apparitions therefore have an important role to play. When we understand their role we ought to welcome them joyfully as God's grace, a light guiding us through the night of faith. If God is disappointed by our indifference and decides to send his Son or Our Lady to repeat, with signs of fire and light, that which we have forgotten, to convert us, to involve us prophetically in the history of salvation, this is indeed Good News, urgent news, marking a turning point for the world. [*The Apparitions of the Blessed Virgin Mary Today*, page 19]

We can then confidently believe in apparitions that have proven authentic and learn from the messages brought to us by Mary. Let us review a few of the most important ones.

In 1531 Mary appeared to Juan Diego, a humble, simple, indigenous man in Mexico. Although not the first apparition of Mary, this is the most famous early one. She presented Herself as Our Lady of Guadalupe and spoke to him in the local Nahuatl language. Guadalupe means "the one who smashed the snake." What a coincidence, don't you think? Mary asked for a church to be built at that site in Her honor, but when Juan Diego went to tell the local bishop, he did not believe him and asked him to prove his claim by some miracle.

Mary appeared again to Juan Diego and asked him to collect flowers and bring them to Her. Juan Diego collected many roses around the Tepeyac hill, a variety which did not grow locally and normally would not bloom in winter. He collected them in his tilma, a garment that was worn at the front like a long apron, or alternatively draped across the shoulders as a cloak, that could be used as a carry-all. Juan Diego took the flowers to Mary, who Herself rearranged them in the tilma and sent him back to the bishop.

When Juan Diego unfolded the tilma to present the flowers to the bishop, the image of Mary was miraculously imprinted in the cloth. This image can still be seen in the sanctuary of Our Lady of Guadalupe in Mexico City. The image has been thoroughly researched by scientists and found to be authentic, containing many exceptional characteristics. The maguey fiber with which the tilma is made will typically disintegrate after twenty or thirty years, but this one is close to five hundred years old and is intact. The fact that amazes me the most is that Mary's eyes reveal minute images of the bishop, and in his eyes is the image of Juan Diego opening the tilma in front of him. With this appearance, Mary ended a long period of human sacrifices, a common practice among the Aztecs, and it proved to the Europeans that Mary was the mother of all.

The next important apparition was in 1830, in Rue de Bac, Paris, France, when Mary appeared to St. Catherine Labouré and showed her the image of a medal that was to be made. This medal, known as the Medal of the Immaculate Conception, also became known as the "Miraculous Medal," because of the many miracles associated with it. The front of the medal shows Mary within an oval frame, standing upon a globe, wearing many rings of different colors, most of which shine rays of light over the globe. St Catherine asked why some of Her rings did not shed light, and Mary reportedly replied "Those are the graces for which people forget to ask." On the frame of the oval are the following words: *O Mary, conceived without sin, pray for us who have recourse to thee.* The back of the medal shows the Immaculate Heart of Mary next to the Sacred Heart of Jesus. This was the first time that both hearts were shown together. This apparition is said to have influenced Pope Pius IX in his definition of the dogma of the Immaculate Conception in 1858.

Later, in 1846 in La Salette, France, Mary appeared to two children and gave many prophecies of calamities that would affect France. She asked for prayers and conversion to avoid these calamities, but eventually these came true. Then, twelve years later, in 1858, on the feast of the Annunciation on March 25th, Mary appeared again in France to Bernadette Soubirous, this time in Lourdes. She presented Herself as the "Immaculate Conception," confirming the dogma established four years earlier. Mary asked Bernadette to dig a hole in the ground, something she immediately did, despite the mocking of the villagers, and soon after, water started to flow out of this hole, which has continued flowing. Many miracles have been reported from people who drink or wash in this water. Mary appeared eighteen or nineteen times to Bernadette.

The apparitions of Mary in Fatima, Portugal, in 1917 to three children coincided with World War I. Mary presented Herself as The Lady of the Rosary and asked them to pray the rosary every day, reiterating many times that the rosary was the key to personal and world peace. Mary appeared six times to the children, and during Her final apparition She announced there was to be a miracle. When the day came, in the presence of 70,000 people, including newspaper reporters and photographers, the sun made movements outside of cosmic laws, amusing the audience. Mary's apparitions in Fatima were very controversial because She asked for the consecration of Russia to Her Immaculate Heart, so that Russia could be saved from communism. Mary also predicted World War II if humans did not change their ways.

At this point it is worth discussing if these apparitions are in fact evidence of the resurrection of Mother Mary. If we understand resurrection as a visible demonstration of life after death, in showing or presenting Herself, Mary is demonstrating that She is alive and well, albeit in spirit. The fact that human beings can see Her and hear Her voice is evidence of Her existence. This is similar to Jesus' resurrection; he appeared out of nowhere and then could be seen and heard. Thomas actually put his fingers in Jesus wounds. With Her hands, Mary actually arranged Juan Diego's flowers.

Between 1945 and 1951 Mary appeared to Ida Peerdeman in Amsterdam, Holland, and made many predictions of events that took place soon after. Mary's apparitions here became know as "Our Lady of All Nations" because of the many messages which involved the conversion of all peoples of the world to God.

Mary has appeared to many people over the last fifty years. For example, Her apparitions in Cairo, Egypt, in the suburb of Zeitoun, were reportedly witnessed by millions of people. The apparitions started in 1968, one year after the Six-day War with Israel, and lasted two or three years. On any given night, there might be 250,000 people gathered around the Coptic Orthodox Church of Saint Mary in Zeitoun. Egyptians and foreigners, including Copts, Eastern Orthodox, Roman Catholics, Protestants, Muslims, Jews, and people of no particular faith, witnessed the events.

Mary did not speak, She simply showed Herself. She would appear on the top of the roof of the church and stay there for hours. Many pictures were taken of Mary during these apparitions, some of them extensively published in newspapers at the time. Through these apparitions, Mary converted many people by Her presence. Through Her silence She delivered a message to people of all faiths, allowing Her presence to be experienced by the heart instead of the mind. Mary often appeared above the church holding an olive branch, an ancient sign of peace. Supernatural doves of light were also observed flying around the domes of the church, another symbol of peace. These apparitions right after the defeat inflicted by Israel may have helped heal many of Egypt's war wounds.

The apparitions at Garabandal, Spain, which started in 1961 and went on through 1965, where Mary is claimed to have appeared over 2,000 times to four children, are interesting because of the interaction that Mary had with the children. During these apparitions, the children would walk in ecstasy across the village, singing and dancing with Mary. She would give them a verse of a song and the children would complete with their own words the next verse of the song.

The timing of the Garabandal apparitions was also very important, coinciding with the missile crisis in Cuba, when nuclear annihilation threatened the world. Garabandal is full of prophetic messages from Mary, and there is still much controversy surrounding these events. Many of Mary's apparitions do coincide with periods of great danger for the world.

The apparitions in Medjugorje, which started in 1981 in this small village in Bosnia-Herzegovina, in what used to be Yugoslavia, announced the great turmoil this country was going to be subject to. The separation of Croatia from Yugoslavia started the most brutal war in Europe since World War II and divided Yugoslavia into several nations, with tremendous loss of life.

Mary appeared to six children practically every day: Ivan, Jakov, Marija, Mirjana, Vicka, and Ivanka. She first appeared at the top of a hill in Medjugorje, then in a church, and later in the homes of the visionaries. The interactions between Mary and the children were ample, as evidenced by the many filmed, documented, and researched cases. Through 2007, it is estimated that more than 10,000 messages have been received by the visionaries. Now all six visionaries are adults, and Mary still appears to three of them daily (Marija, Vicka, and Ivan), once a month to Mirjana, and once a year to Jakov and Ivanka.

It is important to also note that Yugoslavia was home to Islam and Eastern Orthodox religions as well as Roman Catholicism. In Medjugorje, as in Cairo, with Her apparitions, Mary has brought a tolerance and mutual respect for other religions to us. In one of Her messages, Mary said: "You must respect each man's beliefs. No one should despise another for his convictions. God is one and indivisible. It is not God but believers who have caused the dreadful division in the world." In another message, referring to the population of Yugoslavia She said: "...Muslims, Orthodox, and Catholics to my son and myself are all one. You are all my children."

Here is Mary's last message from Medjugorje Web [www.medjugorje.org], at the time of this writing. In it, Mary asks for prayer for Her intentions and asks for us to pray and fast so we may carry out God's will. It could not be more pertinent to the subject of this book.

> Mary's Message of October 25, 2008, from Medjugorje: "Dear children! In a special way I call you all to pray for my intentions so that, through your prayers, you may stop Satan's plan over this world, which is further from God every day, and which puts itself in the place of God and is destroying everything that is beautiful and good in the souls of each of you. Therefore, little children, arm yourselves with prayer and fasting so that you may be conscious of how much God loves you and may carry out God's will. Thank you for having responded to my call." [www.medjugorje.org]

Here is another random message picked from the www.medjugorje.org Web site, to illustrate the simplicity, but profoundness, of Mary's messages.

> Mary's Message of August 25, 2001, from Medjugorje: "Dear children! Today I call all of you to decide for holiness. May for you, little children, always in your thoughts and in each situation, holiness be in the first place, in work and in speech. In this way, you will also put it into practice; little by little, step by step, prayer and a decision for holiness will enter into your family. Be real with yourselves and do not bind yourselves to material things but to God. And do not forget, little children, that your life is as passing as a flower. Thank you for having responded to my call." [www.medjugorje.org]

Other important cases of recent apparitions have been reported in Akita, Japan, in 1973; Betania, Venezuela, between 1974 and 1984; Cuapa, Nicaragua, in 1980; Kibeho, Rwanda, between 1981 and 1983; Damascus, Syria, between 1982 and 1990; San Nicolas, Argentina, between 1983 and 1990; Hroushiv (Grouchevo), Ukraine, between 1986 and 1988; Cuenca, Ecuador, between 1988 and 1990; Las Pavas, El Salvador, since 1992; Hollywood, Florida since 1995. There are many other reported cases of apparitions of Mary in the world these days, which can be researched on the Internet. However, I urge the reader not to try to discover them all but rather to study the most important one of our times: Medjugorje. I highly recommend the books of Wayne Weible, including one of the most popular, *The Final Harvest.* Alternatively, go to www.medjugorje.org/weiblep.htm and read his "Miracle at Medjugorje."

Last summer, Beatriz, who is originally from El Salvador, and I went to Las Pavas Hill in El Salvador to talk to Nelly Hurtado, the visionary who has seen and received messages from Mother Mary since 1992. Nelly is a simple, humble, and intelligent woman who graduated in computer science in Brazil, where she went to study during the civil war in El Salvador. After graduation, she began to work and was ready to get married and permanently reside in Brazil, when she heard the voice of Mary calling her back to El Salvador. Every month since 1992, sometimes twice a month, she has been receiving messages from Mary at the sanctuary of Our Lady of Fatima in Las Pavas Hill.

We spent several hours talking about her life and her messages and how these had changed Nelly's life and had brought about many miracles to those who believed. The messages of Mary in Las Pavas are consistent with those at other apparition sites. They ask for conversion and for prayer of the rosary for peace, and they contain a sense of urgency that has been increasing with time. Nelly explains. Mary will frequently refer to Las Pavas as a future "Beacon of Light" for the world. In 2007, Mary told Nelly that the Church would soon acknowledge Her as Co-Redemptrix. The whole experience was beautiful and allowed me to get closer to one of these special individuals who have the fortune of communicating with Mary.

We also talked about the pictures that have been taken at the site, which show the door of heaven opening up and Mary coming through this door for Her conversations with Nelly. My mother-in-law happens to have been given the privilege of recording these images. She uses a Polaroid camera, which seems to provide the best resolution for these pictures. If I didn't know my mother-in-law, I would probably have the same doubts that you or others may have about these pictures, but because she has taken them, I know them to be real. She has not only taken pictures like these in Las Pavas, but she also recorded the same door in other places of apparition. Please refer to Appendix III to see some of the pictures.

A few days later, still in El Salvador, we were at Beatriz' family's beach house in Costa del Sol. It was Sunday, and we went to a mass in a small chapel, right in front of the beach house property. Fr. Abel, the priest who serves in this church, a good friend of Beatriz' family for a long time, was offering the mass that Sunday. At the end of the mass, right before the blessing, Fr. Abel made a strange remark; he said: "My children, our Blessed Virgin Mother is asking us to prepare, prepare, prepare, because the times that are coming are going to be difficult." There were a few more words, but this was all I could record.

Outside the church, we approached Fr. Abel and asked him why he had made that unusual remark at the end of the mass. He told us that at the end of the mass, he had a vision of Mother Mary and that She told him to pass that message on to the congregation. He thought to himself then that it was not appropriate for a priest to give these types of worrisome messages to people in that way, but Mother Mary insisted, so he went ahead. I believe Mary appeared to Fr. Abel that day because she wanted those words in this book.

He went on to tell us that a carved image of Mary that hangs in the front of the church to the right of the altar had a peculiar history associated with Beatriz' family. He told us that one night under a full moon, about one month earlier, a fisherman was walking by the beach in front of the family beach house and saw the wooden remains of a canoe. Out of curiosity, he turned the piece of the canoe over to find, to his amazement, an image of Mother Mary reflected in the wet sand, with twelve stars around Her head. He was so impressed and joyous at this experience that he took the piece of the canoe with him and carved the image he had seen in the sand that night inside. He then gave the carved image to Fr. Abel.

You may say that these are all coincidences, and they are, but coincidences are happening to us every day. We just do not notice them, because we are not tuned in to that particular energy at that point in our life. For instance, I lived in Caracas, Venezuela, right at the time when Mary was appearing in Betania, between 1974 and 1984. This apparition received the approval of the Church in November 1987, a milestone, because the one prior to that was between 1932 and 1933. I knew this apparition was taking place, but I never took interest in going there or learning more about it. Now that I am writing this book about Mary, I am surrounded by coincidences that bring Mary into my life at all times.

The increase in Marian apparitions in the last few decades is no coincidence. John Kirby, in his work titled "The Day of Mary: The Coming of Mary and Our Mutual Transformation of the World," says the following:

> The Day of Mary has been a 150-year meticulously crafted work of Love. And now the Day is almost complete and the scene has been set, the invitations have been sent out—to all of us—and it is for us to enjoy the life offered and help and share with each other the *how* of a radically new life. (see illustration, page 184)

Mary's presence in the world today is so manifest that it is as if She is installed on Earth right now. But why is She "installed" on Earth? For what purpose? Her messages provide us a clue; consistently during Her apparitions, Mary explains that She is here now because mankind has lost its direction and needs to make changes, or else we will find ourselves in a huge bind.

We really do not need to hear Mary's message to know that mankind is indeed in a big bind. The overpopulation of Earth and our frantic race to destroy our planet should be enough evidence. But apparently we do not comprehend the magnitude of the problem, and Mary is here to try to bring this message home. We are now facing one of the greatest challenges of our history with the global warming of our planet and the inevitable consequences of this. Just look at what happened in New Orleans in 2005 with Hurricane Katrina, with damages exceeding $100 billion dollars, and the 2004 tsunami in the Indian Ocean, which took the lives of 283,000 people.

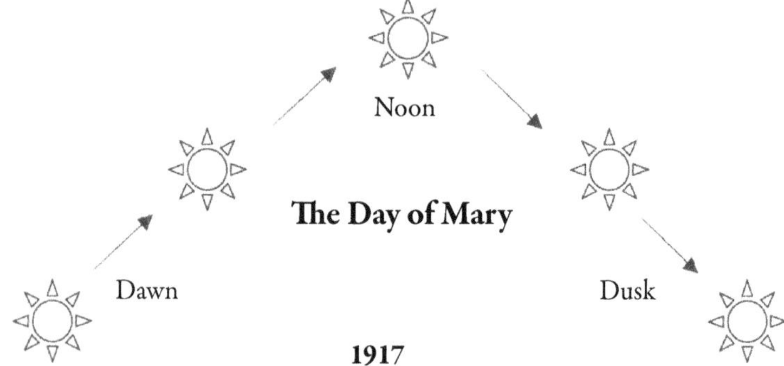

The Day of Mary

1858

Lourdes, Mary appeared 18 or 19 times at dawn or just thereafter

1917

Fatima, 6 appearances just after noon

1961-65

Garabandal, Mary came over 2000 times at any time of day or night, she 'moved in' noon

1981-present

Medjugorje, daily, nearly 10,000 times by late 2007, number becomes almost irrelevant, she always comes in the evening

(Used with permisson from John Kirby.)

Over the last several months as I have been writing this book, the world's financial system has collapsed, destroying with it trillions of dollars of people's wealth. Don't let yourself be fooled by the idea that government bailouts take care of the problem. They might prevent further collapse, but on a collective basis what is lost is gone, and no one or nothing can miraculously bring it back. So we are all poorer, or less wealthy, than we were before. The collapse of the financial system is a severe blow to capitalism; free market economics is the prevailing system in most Western nations. What is there to replace it? We don't know yet. It is too soon to tell, but there will be changes on this front in the future.

In this context of crumbling institutions, environmental problems, financial crisis, and energy crisis, Mary is coming to us with a message of salvation. She is telling us what we need to do to get free of this bind. Unfortunately, very few people have been listening. When Mary and Jesus came to the world two thousand years ago, their immaculate presence raised the consciousness of all mankind. They showed us a path to eliminate suffering in our lives. They assumed the suffering so we would not have to suffer. But what have we done in the last two thousand years with their sacrifice? We, as a collective group, have ignored it! Only few people have lived the path left to us by Mary and Jesus.

Nevertheless, I firmly believe that in the last two thousand years we have made some collective progress, raising our level of consciousness. Today we are collectively better human beings than we were two thousand years ago. We are kinder, less violent, less tolerant of human torture, and we cherish life more. If we have been able to make some spiritual progress in the past, we surely have the capability, the potential, to make much more spiritual progress in the future.

Mary asks for simple things that can help us enormously in this task: prayer and fasting. They are so simple, yet so effective. Prayer and meditation are closely related. The first is more an active communication from us to God. The second is more a passive communication, where we listen to God. Remember, you can pray throughout the day by thanking God for the little things: a beautiful day, the smile of a bypasser. When we don't acknowledge another human being with a smile or a "hello" or a "good day", we are not acknowledging God's presence. Find the time for prayer, but also find the time for meditation so you can listen to God's response.

Try praying the rosary and help bring peace to your heart and to the world. Remember that the rosary is like a mantra, a focused repetition of an intention, lifted to God. He rejoices when we pray in this way and is fast to act upon our requests. If you prefer another mantra, that is fine too.

Prayer and meditation help to purify the body, making each of our subatomic particles vibrate at a higher frequency. Try to further purify your body by fasting at least once a week. Remember that a clean, pure body is where the Holy Spirit likes to reside. The more comfortable we make His temple, the more He will reside in us and the more holy we will become. Let us climb the stairway to heaven one step at a time. The way I like to visualize this is that every time I receive a grace from God, I climb one more step on this stairway. Prayer and fasting are two of the ways in which we can receive graces from God; charity and service are other ways.

Prayer, meditation, and fasting are so simple that it is difficult for us to imagine they can in fact be effective and yield results. Our rational minds cannot fully comprehend this mystical phenomenon, and we end up rejecting or giving up the practice because of its incomprehensible simplicity, which is a triumph of ego that condemns us and the planet. Let's persevere and trust in these mysteries. They will help us to awaken to God—and perhaps one day we will reach enlightenment. At a minimum, they will help ease some of our life pains and dissatisfactions.

When I talk to my friends about relevant issues of life, there is an underlying dissatisfaction in most of them, an emotional and spiritual dissatisfaction, sometimes even frustration; despite achieving financial freedom, the soul is still unhappy. More and more, we find ourselves stretched for time, in a world that seems to be spinning faster everyday. The demands of the world pull us in so many directions that we lose some of our own identity. This increases the feeling of emptiness of the soul. The more we forget who we are, the more we separate from God, the more our soul yearns to find its way back home. This is the feeling of emptiness that we may feel.

I remember from my first corporate experience, which lasted thirteen years, that I felt as if I was living my life in a speeding electric train that constantly circled the Earth. I could look out the window and see there was another world out there, but I was not part of it. I could not get off the train because it never stopped. Everything I needed was in the train: food, sleeping quarters, friends, work, entertainment, etc. I did not need to go out for anything.

One day, when I finally decided to get off the train, after many earlier failed attempts, I had no other recourse but to jump off, with the train still in motion. Needless to say, I hit pretty hard upon landing, because life outside the train was very different. I found myself doing things that you take for granted while in the train. "Who is going to fix my computer? I have to go to the bank myself...Are you kidding?"

It was not easy, and it took me some time to adjust to the different world. Somehow, during all those years, I had allowed my job to change me into something that I was not. Do not let this happen to you in your job, family, friends, or other circles. Most of us do not realize how much we compromise ourselves in our daily lives. It is a gradual process, so we don't notice it much. But believe me, it does happen to everyone to some degree.

Every time we make a decision that compromises our soul, we separate a little more from God. If we are not careful, before we know it, we may be so removed from God that there just is no more light in our souls. This is a very dangerous place to be in. This is the place that our egos love. Our ego will do anything to bring us to a place far from God, starting with making us hungry for the recognition of those close to us, especially friends, co-workers, and family.

When we replace the recognition of God with the recognition of another human being, we are dancing to the tune of our ego and making one of the biggest mistakes in life. The ego becomes like a voracious black hole, sucking in everything in the vicinity. The more it grows, the stronger its power. When Mary tells us to turn to God, She is asking us to cut off the dependency we have on the recognition of other human beings. We are betting the farm on the wrong horse when we bet on the ego. Why do we even need the recognition of another human being, when we can have the recognition of God?

In part, I believe we do this because of our insecurity. Remember doubting Thomas, the Apostle who had to get his fingers into Jesus' wounds before he could believe that Jesus was indeed resurrected in front of him. Our minds and our ego will tell us that we should not place our bets on something we cannot see or touch. It is a lot easier to rely on real people, ego will say. Notice how people who have been distant from God change their lives completely when they come closer to God. They become more spiritual and humble and drop the needs of the ego. The Apostles had such a profound experience of God that they dedicated their lives to preach the teachings of Jesus.

If we could just believe a little more that God is indeed there for us, watching us every minute, perhaps we could begin to impress Him instead of our friends or colleagues. This will satiate our soul's hunger, our soul's emptiness. But this is not enough. There is also the conscious realization that material possessions and technological advances are not rendering the results that we had anticipated. They are not bringing happiness to our lives. We have become the slaves of our material possessions, and we are never satisfied. We always want the latest car, the latest phone, the latest television, and so on. Most of us would not be able to give up our material possessions that we have worked so hard for.

But do we really have to give up our material possessions to be happy? I believe not. The point here is that you have to be wholeheartedly willing to give them up. When we make this conscious decision, we are sending to the universe, to God, a very powerful message; we are sending out our intention that we are willing to trade our possessions for pursuit of happiness, for pursuit of enlightenment. Whether God decides to take these possessions away from us or not is unknown. We must therefore be prepared to accept His decision if it happens before we expect it. That is the risk you are being asked to take.

Are you willing to take this risk to come closer to the perfection of God? Are you willing to "let God and let go"? It is a very difficult decision, one that you must consider carefully. Of the many things discussed in this book, this is perhaps the most difficult one. "Doubt is an essential element of faith," said Kierkegaard. For example, it does not require any faith from you to know that this book exists, because you are touching it and reading it. On the other hand, to believe or have faith in God is to believe in God without perceiving him through your five senses.

From my always rational point of view, I think that if God took material things away from us all, the planet would be filled with vacant, unused properties and things. It would also be filled with lots of people who have nowhere to live, nothing to eat, and no clothing. It just wouldn't make sense, would it? In my experience, and from a material standpoint, I have everything I need and would want to have, but I also believe I do not have many things I do not need. In our house, anything that is not used for a while is given away to charity, to people who really need it. Our house is not cluttered and simple.

The more you get rid of old stuff, the more you open yourself for the new, my smart wife taught me. You have to free space in your life so the universe can provide the things you may be intending for, which don't arrive because there is no space in your life. I say this in a figurative way, but it applies to all aspects of life. You may get rid of an old coat and find that releasing this opens you up to receive an emotional gift you had been craving.

Has God taken material things away from me? Yes, of course He has. One of the more painful ones was the amount of stock I held in my company; after I resigned the CEO position; this was cut in half by a forced dilution executed by our English partners. To see the fruits of your years of work disappear is not a pleasant feeling. God knows what He is doing, and I submit to His wisdom. Time will tell why this happened.

I am one who has difficulty believing blindly and needs to understand things first. It is not that I have to see it to believe it, like doubting

Thomas. But I do need to understand the things I believe in. My curiosity helps me build a stronger faith. My curiosity has led me to this point, where I am now convinced that Jesus and Mary came to life for a very important reason—to save you and me. Through my research, I discovered important elements that have solidified my position. This gives me confidence, gives me the security to deposit my trust in God. I am willing to bet my farm on God's horse today like never before in my life.

I marvel at the turns that my life has taken in the last two years. Our move to Sedona has been such a blessing in our family's life. I cannot explain to you the feeling I get when I look out the window of my office as I write these lines and see the beautiful red rocks. Or the feeling I get on my morning jog on the mountain trail near my home, the sense of peace I have in my heart when I am meditating on one of the red rocks along the trail—a sense of peace that you only get when you know you are flowing freely down the river; at peace with yourself and with everything. This tremendous feeling of gratification you can only find in the trusting flow of a life in God.

Through following Mary's advice, I have been able to arrive at this current state in my life, which is like my own Paradise. By surrendering to His will, offering many prayers of the rosary and a few fasts; through meditation and contemplation; through the overall simplification of my life, as Mary suggests, I have arrived at this marvelous point right now.

Is this the only way? I would never dare to claim so. It is a way that has worked for me and that may work for you as well. Allow Mary, the loving Mother of all, to comfort you as well and to give you the motherly care your soul may be craving for. Forget the differences brought about by men's religions and by divisions imposed by race or beliefs. Mary is the Mother of All Nations, the Mother of All Peoples, the Universal Mother, and She is ready to pour Her love unto you.

Chapter 12

The End of Times, or Ethicalism

In Her messages, Mary is asking us to turn to God, to love Him, to pray, fast, and pray the rosary. She wants us to behave according to the principles outlined by God. It is a way in which we can return to the path of Adam and Eve and find Paradise, one of the ways in which we can find enlightenment. Mary is calling us urgently from many apparition places to move now because there is not much time.

Some of the messages have an apocalyptic tone, making us think that we are at the end of the road. The conditions of the world today suggest that a catastrophe, or several catastrophes, could happen anytime now. Books and movies with examples of events that could happen because of environmental changes, terrorism, or viral disease abound. Then there is the threat of something major happening in the year 2012, according to many sources. Is it possible we are near the end of times as we know them?

In both Garabandal and Medjugorje, Mary spoke about a warning, a miracle, and a punishment. The warning is something that will be sent by God and that all human beings will experience. Then there will be a great miracle, and a sign will remain visible at the sites of apparition. Then the punishment will come, which will depend on the reaction of humanity to the previous events. According to the visionaries, the punishment can be reduced by prayer. It has been done before; through prayer and fasting, people have been able to stop wars and suspend natural laws. Similar messages of punishments to come, brought upon ourselves, if mankind does not rectify its ways have been received at many other apparition sites.

Medjugorje is perhaps the best source of documented information right now, so I will elaborate more on these particular apparitions. In addition to the messages, each of the visionaries is to receive ten secrets; when the tenth secret is revealed, Mary will stop appearing on a daily basis to them. The secrets are future events to take place in the world, some pertaining to the visionaries themselves and their town or city, and others throughout the entire world.

The ninth and tenth secrets relate to a chastisement for the sins of the world. The chastisement can be lessened by prayers and fasting, as happened some years ago, when an evil that threatened the world, according to the seventh secret, was eliminated through prayer and fasting. For that reason Mary said: "You have forgotten that with prayer and fasting you can ward off wars, suspend natural laws."

At the time of this writing Mirjana, Jakov, and Ivanka have received the ten secrets, and Marija, Vicka, and Ivan have received only nine secrets. Only one secret has been allowed to be revealed so far, and it has to do with a supernatural, indestructible, and visible sign that will appear on the mountain where Mary first appeared in Medjugorje. This sign is for the purpose of convincing those who do not yet believe in God.

Once Mary delivers the tenth secret to all visionaries, there will be three warnings, visible occurrences, given to the world. Mirjana will be made aware ten days before each of the warnings and be required to pray and fast for seven days with a priest of her choice. Then, three days before the warning is to occur, the priest will announce to the world what, where, and when the warning is to take place. The three warnings will take place within a brief period of time. After the three warnings have been delivered, the permanent sign will be left on the Medjugorje hill. Mary says there is little time left and calls for urgent conversion and reconciliation. [www.medjugorje.org]

The message from Medjugorje is a grave matter and concerns all of us and the world. Are we close to the end of times? Do we know when it will happen? From the message itself, it seems that these events will take place during Mirjana's lifetime, who at the time of this writing in 2008 is forty-three years old.

> Mary's Message of October 25, 2006, from Medjugorje: "Dear children! Today the Lord permitted me to tell you again that *you live in a time of grace*. You are not conscious, little children, that God is giving you a great opportunity to convert and to live in peace and love. You are so blind and attached to earthly things and think of earthly life. God sent me to lead you toward eternal life. I, little children, am not tired, although I see that your hearts are heavy and tired for everything that is a grace and a gift. Thank you for having responded to my call." [www.medjugorje.org]

Is it possible then that all these apparitions of Mary are preceding Christ and that we are at the doorsteps of His second coming? It is quite possible, but at the same time we have to remember that Saint Paul himself thought that Jesus' second coming would happen during his lifetime. Nobody really knows when this will happen, and if Saint Paul erred by two thousand years, we could easily err for many years as well. It is better not to try to find or fix a date for this event.

On the other hand, we have to make some changes now in our lives and in our world if our goal is to walk the path back to Paradise, to take back the stairway to heaven, as Led Zeppelin so eloquently said in that great song. We need to make changes for us to reach enlightenment, to be full of grace again, and to rescue ourselves from pain and suffering. Positive changes will not only improve our lives but also quench our souls' thirst for God.

Are we not thirsty for God? Each one of us will manifest this thirst in different ways. Even non-believers are thirsty for wholeness and are missing something in their lives. There is something that is not working in our society right now, the result of separation from universal peace and love, if you will. Many things have contributed to this state of affairs, but there is one aspect of our society that is perhaps at the core of the problem—one aspect that if we don't change, we won't be able to make collective progress. This is the concept of Growth.

Yes, many of our problems begin with an ingrained structural concept of Growth in our society. For the last several thousand years, mankind has lived under the concept of growth: "more is better." When the population of the world was lower, growth in population was perceived as a strength, because it brought with it growth in the economy. In the last one hundred years, though, the concept of growth has reached its maximum, and it is now time for it to give way to another concept. Perhaps the concept of Stability, or the concept of "less is better."

The concept of growth worked well for us for many thousands of years, but it no longer helps. On the contrary, it is the source of many of our problems. Let's look at the business world, for example; growth has created a sad reality that is affecting us all today. Corporate Chief Executive Officers (CEOs) have a very clear duty or mission ahead of any others, and that is to look after the investment of the shareholders and provide attractive returns on investment (ROI). Our society is governed by the ROI. Newspapers and business magazines, as well as television programs, are constantly pouring out tons of statistics and rankings to help us quickly identify the best ROIs.

We, as consumers, in our desire for increasing returns on our investments, have created a pervasive system that leads corporations to do exactly the things that we then complain about. CEOs are faced with making decisions that may not be the best for the environment, for example, because they need to reach their profit targets. Wall Street is unforgiving to CEOs who miss their profit forecasts. Then, as consumers, we complain about the environmental effects of these decisions, even when we hold stock in these corporations through our pensions or mutual fund investments. Many cases of fraudulent actions have been made in corporations in the last years because of the need to show good financial numbers to Wall Street and the shareholders.

This is a problem that we need to address. We need to replace the mentality of the ROI with a new mentality. This new mentality should include some measure of ethical behavior. Suppose we created something like a CEI, the Corporate Ethical Index. Companies would be ranked according to CEI, and consumers should invest in those corporations with the highest CEIs. The incentive mechanism for the business world would change to one that encompasses important aspects of business and social ethics. The end no longer justifies the means. Now, the means are equally, if not more, important. The CEI would be, in a sense, a measure of the "holiness" of a corporation. For more information on the CEI, please refer to Appendix IV.

> Mary's Message of May 25, 2006 from Medjugorje: "Dear children! Also today I call you to put into practice and to live my messages that I am giving you. Decide for *holiness*, little children, and think of heaven. Only in this way, will you have peace in your heart that no one will be able to destroy..." [www.medjugorje.org]

Capitalism is out of steam! It needs to be replaced by a new order based on ethics: "Ethicalism," as I will start calling it here. Mary's message to the world is precisely this one. We need to return to ethics and good, moral common sense. We need more holiness. There are too many things that are just not right and cannot take us anyplace good. It has to start with each one of us, in our personal lives, in our homes and families. We must guard against judgment as we do this, because there are many people in the world with different opinions on issues of all sorts, and they deserve to be respected. We have to simplify our lives and begin to consider that more is not always better.

Simplifying Our Lives

Mary wants us to simplify our lives and become like children. Most people who have attained high levels of spiritual development live simple lives. Even if they are wealthy and powerful, they live simple lives. Think about Mahatma Gandhi, who, being the major political and spiritual leader of India, lived the simplest life you could imagine. Gandhi called it "reducing himself to zero," which entailed giving up unnecessary expenditure and embracing a simple lifestyle.

Think also about Mother Theresa, another excellent contemporary example of someone who lived a simple life; all her belongings could be packed in a small suitcase or box. Mother Teresa's Missionaries of Charity at the time of her death were operating 610 missions in 123 countries. What an exceptional accomplishment. Simplicity does not mean that you will live meaningless lives, as is well exemplified by these two examples. We can all simplify our lives if we really want to. This is something very much in our control.

> Message of Our Lady given through Mirjana, September 02, 2007: "...Give me your *simple hearts*, purified by fasting and prayer. Only in the *simplicity of your hearts* is your salvation..." [www.medjugorje.org]

> Message of Our Lady given through Mirjana, May 02, 2008: "By God's will I am here with you in this place. I desire for you to open your hearts to me and to accept me as a mother. With my love I will teach you *simplicity* of life and richness of mercy and I will lead you to my Son..." [www.medjugorje.org]

Beatriz and I wanted to simplify our lives, and we knew the first step was to get out of Miami. We wanted to move to a quieter city, to a place where the cost of living would be lower. Only then would I be able to afford to leave my job, which was not compatible with the lifestyle that Mary had imprinted in my heart. By selling our house in Miami, we could afford to buy a similar house for about half the price in other places in the United States. We could then put the extra cash received from the equity we had built on the house in the bank and use it to cover expenses.

The cost of living in Miami had gone up tremendously as a result of the exponential growth of the city and of the increased costs brought about by the hurricanes. We are now paying twelve times less in taxes and insurance on our house, since moving to Sedona. We are paying about one-fourth of what we were paying in gas, despite the higher price of gasoline, because we live in a small city, where distances are shorter and there is no traffic. Most things are cheaper here compared to Miami.

Moving to a small city helped us simplify our lives by removing huge financial pressures from my back. The lifestyle of a small city compared to the hectic lifestyle of Miami also led to simplification in other areas. We find ourselves spending more time in nature than in the mall; entertaining more often in the safety and comfort of our home instead of in Miami Beach's questionable ambience; contemplating more, with a greater sense of overall peace.

It is very necessary in the world today for people and families to spend some time in tranquility, some time in silence. Because of all the noise around us and our hectic lifestyles, we have separated so far from God. There is no time for quiet meditation, for contemplation, for prayer, for silence. It has been replaced by the many media distractions that surround us, by cell phones and all sorts of electronic devices that do not allow us to disconnect from the world. People get upset or anxious if we do not pick up their calls or text messages immediately, as if we are doing something wrong when we don't answer.

We have mortgaged our lives to acquire more of what is not needed. In the frantic pursuit of this "more," we have no time left for our souls, for our relationship with God. Our mind, or ego, is extremely happy because it has managed to separate us and gain control of our lives now. Ego defines our life by the goals we set for ourselves: "I need a larger house," "I need a better car," "I need..."

If we change our goals, we can change our lives. What if your goal was simply to keep the things you have, or even downsize? What if you decided to move to a smaller house, acquire a less expensive car, and get rid of one of the four television sets you have in your house? If your financial demands went down, wouldn't your stress in life also go down? I think the way of the future is "less is better," rather than "more is better."

We always like to blame other people or the government for our maladies. It's human nature. I am trying to impress on you that there is so much that is in our control. If we stop buying the products of a company that harms the environment, we show our power. If we use a three-year-old phone, we show our power. If we move to a smaller house, we show our power. We begin to be in control of our life, as opposed to being controlled by life.

As we regain control of our lives, we will find more time for introspection, for play and family life. We will be more effective at pulling our own children out of the electronic world. As we start to focus more on simplicity and less on what our neighbor has, we will feel relaxed and gain new freedom. We no longer have to impress anyone but God. What a feeling, what a relief! The next time you catch yourself trying to impress your peers, your friend, your family, stop yourself right there and ask, "Who am I kidding! Why would I want to impress this person, instead of impressing God?"

> Mary's Message of November 25, 2007 from Medjugorje: "Dear children! Today, when you celebrate Christ, the King of all that is created, I desire for Him to be the King of your lives. Only through giving, little children, can you comprehend the gift of Jesus' sacrifice on the Cross for each of you. Little children, *give time to God* that He may transform you and fill you with His grace, so that you may be a grace for others. For you, little children, I am a gift of grace and love, which comes from God for this peaceless world. Thank you for having responded to my call." [www.medjugorje.org]

You are probably familiar with the "Hundredth Monkey" story and its evolutionary lesson. For those who aren't, here is a brief recount of the story. There was a Japanese monkey species that lived on an island and was being fed sweet potatoes by Japanese scientists in 1952. The monkeys liked the sweet potatoes but did not like the dirt that came with the sweet potatoes. One day a smart monkey had the spark of intelligence to wash the sweet potato in a nearby stream. The smart monkey then taught several other monkeys how to wash the sweet potatoes, and in a few years, most of the monkeys on the island had adopted the new skill.

The amazing part of the story is that in 1958 something extraordinary happened. One day, practically at the same time, monkeys in colonies on other islands that had never been exposed to this feat started washing the sweet potatoes at the same time. It was not a gradual learning process as it had been on the first island, but a sudden collective adoption of a skill that had never been part of their lives before. What made the monkeys on the other islands take this evolutionary step? The explanation, confirmed by several other examples in nature, is that once a certain number of individuals of a given species learn a new skill, they reach the "tipping point"; then the whole species immediately adopts it.

What is not known is how many individuals are necessary to reach the tipping point for the evolutionary leap to occur. What is also not known is whether this process also applies to the human species. There is no reason to believe it would not. With humans so easily influenced by fashions and trends, one would think we are perhaps more prone to this phenomenon than other species. If the Hundredth-Monkey phenomenon also applies to human beings, then when a sufficient number of human beings begin to value the concept of "less is better" and adopt Ethicalism as a way of living, then perhaps our whole species can take an evolutionary leap of consciousness.

I am not a doomsday person, and I believe the chastisement can be avoided. As mentioned earlier, I believe that Mary is reminding us, in a very assertive way, of the need to change and telling us that if we don't change, many beautiful things we currently have will be taken away. The way things are going, if we do not change voluntarily, Mother Earth will force us to change. Mary is telling us that God wants the conversion of each and every one of us and that we are all important for His great plan for the world.

> Mary's Message of June 25, 2007, from Medjugorje: "Dear children! Also today, with great joy in my heart, I call you to conversion. Little children, do not forget that *you are all important* in this great plan, which God leads through Medjugorje. *God desires to convert the entire world* and to call it to salvation and to the way towards Himself, who is the beginning and the end of every being. In a special way, little children, from the depth of my heart, I call you all to open yourselves to this great grace that God gives you through my presence here. I desire to thank each of you for the sacrifices and prayers. I am with you and I bless you all. Thank you for having responded to my call." [www.medjugorje.org]

Once we achieve a higher level of consciousness as a species, we will be one step closer to Paradise, which is still "out there," as Anne Catherine Emmerich expressed. Physicists have been able to come up with clever theories that explain how the universe works; the parallel universes theory is among them. I am not a physicist and their theories are beyond my level of understanding, but it is possible that some of these parallel universes exist at a higher level of energetic vibrations, just as radio, television, and cell phone waves are all around us, but invisible. Maybe the higher vibration frequency universe is just around us, but we don't see it either.

I mentioned earlier that my mother-in-law takes pictures on the apparition site of Mother Mary in El Salvador. These pictures, presented in Appendix III, show what may be impossible to describe in words. They show the door of heaven opening as Mary emerges, and they show a horizontal line of what appears to be another dimension. One of the most remarkable pictures I have seen shows two pyramidal structures in golden color that could be structures in another dimension. These pyramidal structures float in the air in front of the trees. Perhaps one day, scientists with enough curiosity may understand why these pictures are captured so eloquently with Polaroid film.

It is quite possible that if we increase our consciousness, our awareness, we may transcend to one of these parallel universes and "cast ourselves out of this world" and back into Paradise. Recall how Adam and Eve were expelled or cast out of Paradise? Where did they go to when they left Paradise? They went to another world that vibrated at a lower frequency, which is the world in which we live today. Mary is here now to take all of us back to Paradise. No one needs to be left behind; we just need to achieve a critical mass of enlightened individuals, who are living according to God's will.

We are all living a dream, an illusion, while in this world. Our life does not end with death. Death is just a transition point, when we shed our body to return to the light beings, the spiritual beings, we really are. Quantum physics has proven that our bodies and our surroundings, including the Earth and the universe, is mostly empty space. Everything is mostly empty space, the things we touch, the things we see, and all the things we perceive through our five senses. The complexity of our mind is such that it can conjure or create a scenario in which we exist and experience life the way our minds want us to. The collective creation of the six billion minds inhabiting the Earth today is what is giving the world the form we perceive and experience.

As each of these individual minds begin to comprehend that we are a product of our own imagination, and that if we change our thoughts we also change our perception of reality, our existence, then mankind, will begin to change. This process is already well in motion. Hundreds of thousands of people in the world today have already incorporated this vital piece of information into their conscious minds. Many of these people, through their intentions in prayers and meditations, including the rosary for peace, are already changing the world for all of us. Mary asks us to pray for holiness and peace, and this is exactly what She is referring to.

> Mary's Message of June 25, 2006, from Medjugorje: "Dear children! With great joy in my heart *I thank you for all the prayers* that, in these days, you offered for my intentions. Know, little children,

> that you will not regret it, neither you nor your children. God will reward you with great graces and you will merit eternal life. I am near you and thank all those who, through these years, have accepted my messages, have poured them into their life and decided for *holiness and peace*. Thank you for having responded to my call." [www.medjugorje.org]

Scientific progress is bringing us back to God. Science in the past separated us from God, but not anymore. The breakthrough knowledge and understanding of quantum physics and its implications for how we humans perceive reality cannot be overestimated. We collectively change our thoughts, and we can collectively change the world. However, to change our collective thoughts, we first have to change our individual thoughts.

So what happens to the world as we know it when we move back to Paradise? The answer to this question is that it does not matter; it is not relevant anymore. The world as we know it, including the stars we see in the firmament, is a product of our collective mind creation. Once we start thinking of a different world, the old world is replaced in our living experience by the new world. Just like Paradise is still "out there," the old world would be still "out there" when we look at it from Paradise. It is possible we may return to this world any time, just by distancing and separating again from God. It is possible that the old world may also be the place for those monkeys that refused to wash their sweet potatoes. We know there are a few of those as well among us.

One of the theories of why the ancient Mayan civilization disappeared suddenly and mysteriously from history is that they achieved a level of consciousness that allowed them to transcend to another world. During the ninth century, the Maya centers of civilization were suddenly abandoned, and the large-scale architectural projects and monumental inscriptions halted. The remaining Maya then fell into a long period of decline that persisted until the Spaniards landed in America; we know the rest of the story. It would seem as if the people who had the knowledge suddenly left, while others who did not have this knowledge were left behind. Other theories point to possible ecological disasters, climate change, and epidemic diseases.

The Maya had achieved an incredible level of knowledge and progress before their collapse. They were master architects; they had writing; they were exceptional artists and had a deep knowledge of mathematics. The knowledge they had of astronomy baffles scientist today. You have to place things in context; when the Maya were predicting that on December 21, 2012, the winter equinox of that year, the sun was going to be in the center of our Milky Way galaxy, our best "modern" minds were still thinking that the sun was the center of the universe. People who would dare dispute this concept were being burned at the stake still in the fourteenth century.

Are we prepared for this evolution in consciousness, to putting an end to our separation from God? Do we have a genuine desire to transcend to higher vibration planes, where we can find Paradise? While it seems an obvious decision, it is not a simple one. Not everyone is prepared to leave their current lifestyle. People who are already living simple lives or who have little may be more ready to leave everything behind. This decision is more difficult for those strongly attached to material things.

> How hardly shall they that have riches enter into the kingdom of God! For it is easier for a camel to go through a needle's eye, than for a rich man to enter into the kingdom of God. [Luke 18:24–25]

Here is what Beatriz and I do on this front. We consecrate ourselves to Mary every morning; we offer our material wealth, health, and family to Her and to the grace of God. It is important to do this first thing in the morning, because otherwise it doesn't get done. If you place God first in your lives, then things will fall into place, and you will be rewarded throughout the day. You will find yourself rushing less, with less stress, and have much more patience to face the day.

Consecration to Mary

The way we offer the consecration to Mary came naturally to Beatriz in a meditation and was subsequently confirmed and enhanced through our readings. Beatriz' consecration encompasses the offering of her physical, mental, emotional, and spiritual bodies, along with her free will, to Mary. After reading St. Louis de Montfort's "True Devotion to Mary," we confirmed how important it is to consecrate ourselves to Mary.

The consecration I use now goes something like this:

> I consecrate to You, most Holy Mother, knowing that in doing so I am pleasing and also consecrating myself to Jesus. I know that You will take this consecration, and, with your embellishment, love, and purification, You will present it to the Father, who loves You so much and listens so attentively to You.
>
> I consecrate my whole body to You, Mother; I consecrate my five senses to You: sight, hearing, touch, smell, and taste; I consecrate my thinking mind and all its thoughts, specially those good thoughts; I consecrate my heart and all its feelings, specially those happy feelings; I consecrate to You my spirit and my soul.
>
> I consecrate to You, my dear Mother, all my possessions, including my house, my cars, my bank accounts, all my electronic gadgets, my home furnishings and clothing—everything I have. I consecrate to You my work and all good that has come from it; and I consecrate to you my children.
>
> My sweet Mother, I am all Yours, including my free will. Please allow me the wisdom to know what God's will is in my life and the courage to follow it.

De Montfort's consecration is more religiously correct, but more complicated for me to remember and repeat. I have included de Montfort's consecration in Appendix V for your benefit, because I am sure that some people will be delighted to use it.

What the consecration does is offer ourselves up to our Lord, in all aspects, not just the materialistic one, as we have been discussing. It makes us better disposed to listen to God and to follow His will. When we offer our material possessions to God, we allow the universe to make better use of these, and the result is usually better.

Abraham, following God's will, became a very wealthy man. His wealth was passed on for generations, including to Isaac and Jacob. Jacob's son Joseph, who continued the lineage, was sold as a slave by his brothers and ended up in Egypt, without any material possessions or his freedom. But not long after, being loyal to God, he became very wealthy and the most important advisor to the Pharaoh. King Solomon, by doing the same, became the richest man of his time; along with him, the Israelites experienced their most glorious period.

History is full of examples of goodness and material blessings bestowed by God on people that do good, that do His will. God wants us to succeed, to do good, to spread the goodness to the world.

> Mary's Message of February 25, 2006, from Medjugorje: "Dear children! In this Lenten time of grace, I call you to open your hearts to the gifts that God desires to give you. Do not be closed, but with prayer and renunciation say 'yes' to God and *He will give to you in abundance*. As in springtime the earth opens to the seed and yields a hundredfold, so also your heavenly Father will give to you in abundance. I am with you and love you, little children, with a tender love. Thank you for having responded to my call." [www.medjugorje.org]

The Parable of the Talents in Matthew 25:14–30 is perhaps one of the best examples of how God wants us to manage wealth, one that I have used many times in the last years to explain this concept to friends. It goes like this: The master gave each of three servants some gold, in proportion to their abilities. He gave the first one five talents (a measure of gold), the second one two talents, and the third one just one talent. Then he went away for a long period of time and told them to take care of his gold. Some unspecified time later, he returned and asked each servant what they had done with their talents.

The first one explained that he invested his five talents and made five more. The master was happy for him and told him that he would be with him and give him greater riches. The second one explained that he had also invested his two talents and made two more talents. Again, the master rewarded him, telling him he would be by his side and offer him greater riches. The third man explained that he was scared of the master and scared of losing the money, so he dug a hole and hid the talent in the ground, and then he returned the single talent to the master. The master is upset with this servant and punishes him, casting him away from his kingdom, and he gave the talent of the third man to the first man.

God, represented in the master, rewards the servants who put the talents to good use and punishes the one who did not put it to good use. Notice that the punished servant did not steal nor use the talent in a bad way at all. In God's eyes, his fault was not trying. It is significant that God gives the one talent of the third servant to the first servant. God will invest His wealth in those people that give Him the highest return on His spiritual investment. God does not despise wealth. He created wealth. Why would He despise something He created? He wants us to be wealthy so we can do His work on Earth. So don't be afraid of consecrating your wealth to Him directly, or, as I do, through Mary.

The Parable of the Talents is my favorite in the Bible because it explains so many things. Substitute talent, a measure of wealth, with your gifts, your abilities—those things you know you are good at. Perhaps your ability to work with numbers, or your ability to sing, or to run fast, or maybe your ability to design beautiful homes, or to cook wonderful dishes. What are you doing with the talents endowed to you by God? Do you realize these talents belong to Him? When you meet the Master again and He asks you, "What have you done with the talents I gave you? Have you put them to good use?", what will you answer?

I hope your answer will please God when the time comes. I hope your talents have produced good fruit and that God will be pleased. I hope you will be able to say:

> "I delight to do thy will, O my God." [40th Psalm, Verse 8]

With this, we come to the end of this journey. I hope that I have been able to provide you with some insight, that I may have been able to use my talents in an effective way and bring you closer to God. How your relationship with the Universal Mother continues is only up to you. I can tell you this, though: Mary is there for you and me, for everyone, white and black and all those in between. She is there for the Jews, the Muslims, the Buddhists—for all religions. She is there for men and women. She is there for the old, the young, and the children. Mary is there waiting for each one of us. As She said in one of Her messages to Linda Dillon, a good friend of mine: "I will not rest until I have reached each one of you, even if that means that I have to be in every house, in every living room." So let us open our hearts to Mary; let Her carry us in Her precious arms to console and comfort us as the sweet and loving Mother She is.

Appendix I

The Rosary

The word rosary means "crown of roses." Mary explains that each time we say a "Hail Mary," we give Her a beautiful rose and that each complete rosary makes Her a crown of roses. The rosary is considered a perfect prayer, because within its mysteries we relive the lives of Jesus and Mary and earn our Redemption.

The Prayer

The rosary is a circular string of beads divided into five decades of ten small beads; each decade is separated from the next by a larger bead. For each small bead, pray a "Hail Mary," and for each large bead, pray the "Our Father." Each decade represents a mystery or event in the life of Jesus. There are four sets of "Mysteries of the Rosary," and these are prayed on different days as follows:

The Joyful Mysteries are prayed on Mondays and Saturdays
The Sorrowful Mysteries are prayed on Tuesdays and Fridays
The Glorious Mysteries are prayed on Wednesdays and Sundays
The Luminous Mysteries are prayed on Thursdays

Before starting to pray each decade, announce the corresponding Mystery on the large bead. Then, as you pray the following ten "Hail Marys", meditate on the corresponding Mystery. (At the end of this Appendix is the full list of Mysteries.)

In addition to the circular string, a Crucifix is joined to one of the five larger beads by one large bead, which is followed by three smaller beads. These are prayed before the circular string as follows: The "Sign of the Cross" to open; the "Apostle's Creed" is said on the Crucifix; the "Our Father" is said on the large bead; the "Hail Mary" is said on each of the three small beads. There are no Mysteries associated with these prayers, which are the introductory prayers before the decades.

After the introductory prayers and after each decade, say a "Glory Be to the Father." In June 13, 1917, in Fatima, Mary asked that an additional prayer be added after each decade of the rosary (not the introductory prayers). The "Fatima Prayer" is a prayer of forgiveness to Jesus and an intercession for the souls of the departed said after the "Glory Be to the Father." At the end of the fifth decade's "Fatima Prayer," say the "Hail Holy Queen," and repeat the sign of the cross to conclude the rosary.

The Sign of the Cross

In the name of the Father, the Son, and the Holy Spirit. Amen.

Prayer Before the Rosary

After the sign of the cross, you may open your rosary prayer with whatever inspires your heart, including your intentions, but remember to include Mary's intentions for peace for the world and the conversion of all people.

The Our Father

Our Father, who art in heaven, hallowed be Thy name; Thy kingdom come; Thy will be done on Earth as it is in Heaven. Give us this day our daily bread, and forgive us our trespasses as we forgive those who trespass against us; and lead us not into temptation, but deliver us from evil. Amen.

The Hail Mary

Hail Mary, full of grace! The Lord is with thee; blessed are thou among women, and blessed is the fruit of thy womb, Jesus. Holy Mary, Mother of God, pray for us sinners now and at the hour of our death. Amen.

Glory Be to the Father

Glory be to the Father, and to the Son, and to the Holy Spirit. As it was in the beginning, is now, and ever shall be, world without end. Amen.

The Fatima Prayer

O My Jesus, forgive us our sins, save us from the fires of hell, take all souls to Heaven, and help especially those most in need of Your mercy.

The Apostles' Creed

I believe in God, the Father Almighty, Creator of Heaven and Earth; and in Jesus Christ His only Son, Our Lord; who was conceived by the Holy Spirit, born of the Virgin Mary, suffered under Pontius Pilate, was crucified, died, and was buried. He descended into Hell; the third day He arose again from the dead; He ascended into Heaven, and is seated at the right hand of God, the Father Almighty; from thence He shall come to judge the living and the dead. I believe in the Holy Spirit, the Holy Catholic Church, the communion of Saints, the forgiveness of sins, the resurrection of the body, and life everlasting. Amen.

Hail Holy Queen

Hail! Holy Queen, Mother of Mercy, our life, our sweetness and our hope. To you do we cry, poor banished children of Eve. To you do we send up our sighs, mourning and weeping in this valley of tears. Turn then, O most gracious advocate, your eyes of mercy towards us; and after this our exile, show unto us the blessed fruit of your womb, Jesus. O clement! O loving! O sweet Virgin Mary!

Pray for us, O Holy Mother of God, that we may be made worthy of the promises of Christ.

The Mysteries

The Joyful Mysteries

(Said on Mondays and Saturdays)

First Joyful Mystery: The Annunciation of Gabriel to Mary
I Desire the Love of Humility
Think of...
The humility of the Blessed Virgin when the Angel Gabriel greeted Her with these words: "Hail full of grace." [Luke 1:26]

Second Joyful Mystery: The Visitation of Mary to Elizabeth
I Desire Charity Toward my Neighbor
Think of...
Mary's charity in visiting Her cousin Elizabeth and remaining with her for three months before the birth of John the Baptist. [Luke1:39]

Third Joyful Mystery: The Birth of Jesus
I Desire Detachment from Material Things
Think of...
Poverty, so lovingly accepted by Mary when She placed the Infant Jesus, our God and Redeemer, in a manger in the stable of Bethlehem. [Luke 2:1]

Fourth Joyful Mystery: The Presentation of Jesus in the Temple

I Desire Purity of Heart and Body

Think of...

Mary's obedience to the law of God in presenting the Child Jesus in the Temple. [*Luke 2:22]*

Fifth Joyful Mystery: Finding Jesus in the Temple

I Desire to Find the Glory of God

Think of...

The deep sorrow with which Mary sought the Child Jesus for three days, and the joy with which She found Him in the midst of the Teachers of the Temple. [Luke 2:41]

The Sorrowful Mysteries

(Said on Tuesdays and Fridays)

First Sorrowful Mystery: Agony of Jesus in the Garden

I Desire True Repentance for My Sins

Think of...

Our Lord Jesus in the garden of Gethsemane, suffering a bitter agony for our sins. [Matthew 26:36]

Second Sorrowful Mystery: Jesus is Scourged at the Pillar

I Desire a Spirit of Mortification

Think of...

The cruel scourging at the pillar that our Lord suffered; the heavy blows that tore His flesh. [Matthew 27:26]

Third Sorrowful Mystery: Jesus is Crowned with Thorns

I Desire Moral Courage.

Think of...

The crown of sharp thorns that was forced upon our Lord's Head and the patience with which He endured the pain for our sins. [Matthew 27:27]

Fourth Sorrowful Mystery: Jesus Carries his Cross

I Desire the Virtue of Patience

Think of...

The heavy Cross, so willingly carried by our Lord, and ask Him to help you to carry your crosses without complaint. [Matthew 27:32]

Fifth Sorrowful Mystery: The Crucifixion of Jesus

I Desire the Grace of Final Perseverance

Think of...

The love which filled Christ's Sacred Heart during His three-hour agony on the Cross, and ask Him to be with you at the hour of death. [Matthew 27:33]

The Glorious Mysteries

(Said on Wednesdays and Sundays)

First Glorious Mystery: The Resurrection of Jesus

I Desire a Strong Faith

Think of...

Christ's glorious triumph when, on the third day after His death, He arose from the tomb and for forty days appeared to His Blessed Mother and to His disciples. [John 20:1]

Second Glorious Mystery: The Ascension of Jesus

I Desire the Virtue of Hope

Think of...

The Ascension of Jesus Christ, forty days after His glorious Resurrection, in the presence of Mary and His disciples. [Luke 24:36]

Third Glorious Mystery: The Descent of the Holy Spirit at Pentecost

I Desire the Virtue of Wisdom in the Eyes of God

Think of...

The descent of the Holy Spirit upon Mary and the Apostles, in the form of tongues of fire, in fulfillment of Christ's promise. [Acts 2:1]

Fourth Glorious Mystery: The Assumption of Mary into Heaven

I Desire the Grace of a Holy Death

Think of...

The glorious Assumption of Mary into Heaven, when She was united with Her Divine Son.

Fifth Glorious Mystery: The Coronation of Mary as Queen of Heaven and Earth

I Desire a Greater Love for the Blessed Virgin Mary

Think of...

The glorious crowning of Mary as Queen of Heaven by Her Divine Son, to the great joy of all the Saints.

The Luminous Mysteries

(Said on Thursdays)

First Luminous Mystery: The Baptism of Jesus in the River Jordan

And a voice came from the heavens, saying, "This is my beloved Son, with whom I am well pleased." [Matthew 3:17]

Second Luminous Mystery: The Wedding at Cana, Christ Manifested

Jesus did this miracle as the first of his signs in Cana in Galilee and so revealed his glory, and his disciples began to believe in him. [John 2:11]

Third Luminous Mystery: The Proclamation of the Kingdom of God

Jesus came to Galilee proclaiming the gospel of God: "This is the time of fulfillment. The kingdom of God is at hand. Repent, and believe in the gospel." [Mark 1:15]

Fourth Luminous Mystery: The Transfiguration of Jesus

And he was transfigured before them; his face shone like the sun and his clothes became white as light. [Matthew 17:2]

Fifth Luminous Mystery: The Last Supper, the Holy Eucharist

While they were eating, Jesus took bread, said the blessing, broke it, and giving it to his disciples said, "Take and eat; this is my body." Then he took a cup, gave thanks, and gave it to them, saying, "Drink from it, all of you, for this is my blood of the covenant, which will be shed on behalf of many for the forgiveness of sins." [Matthew 26:26][1]

1 The Luminous Mysteries were added by Pope John Paul II on 2002, but no "fruits of the mystery" or "meditations" were defined. I use: God's gift of baptism as a grace for the first myster; Mary's role as Advocate for us before God for the second; Following God's will for the third; Belief in Mary's apparitions for the fourth; Belief in the grace of the Eucharist to bring us closer to Paradise, to eternal life, for the fifth.

Appendix II

Anne Catherine Emmerich's Genealogical Chart

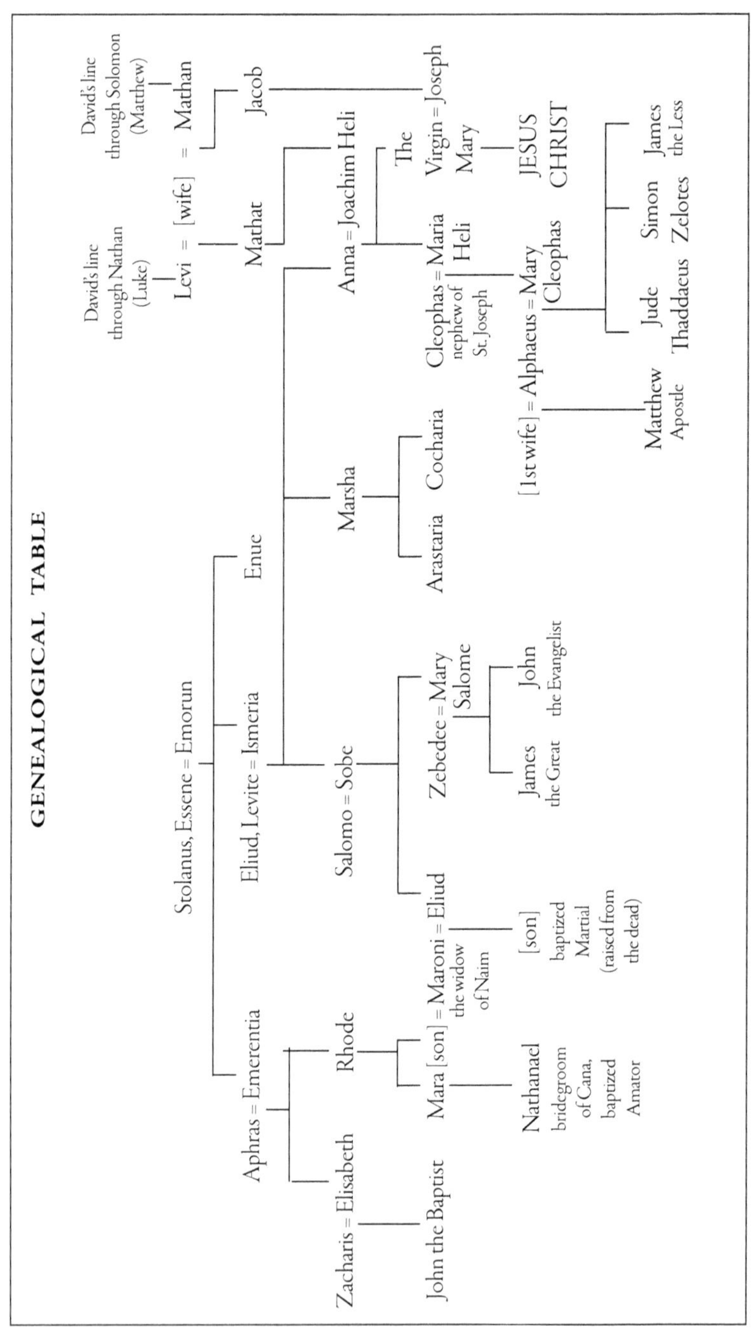

The Genealogical Chart in Appendix II, printed with permission of Tan Books and Publishers, Inc., Rockford, Illinois 61105 from *The Life of The Blessed Virgin Mary From the Visions of Ven. Anne Catherine Emmerich*, from page 384.

Appendix III

Pictures from Cerro Las Pavas

Photo taken by Bertha Marina Salazar in Cerro Las Pavas, El Salvador on May 13, 2005. Nelly Hurtado, the seer that sees and receives Mary's messages, is in ecstasy, while circles of light appear descending onto her.

Photo taken by Bertha Marina Salazar in Cerro Las Pavas, El Salvador on November 25, 1999 showing the door of heaven opening up? The background is trees and sky.

Photo taken by Bertha Marina Salazar in Cerro Las Pavas, El Salvador on March 25, 2002 showing the door of heaven and a figure like Mary coming out, with something like a stairway in the back? The background is trees.

Photo taken by Bertha Marina Salazar in Cerro Las Pavas, El Salvador on February 11, 2003 showing the door of heaven with a figure already outside the door and a horizontal line as a dimensional break?

Photo taken by Bertha Marina Salazar in Cerro Las Pavas, El Salvador in the year 2006 showing two glass type pyramidal structures in between the trees and a left vertical line?

Appendix IV

Corporate Ethical Index: CEI

CEI, the "Corporate Ethical Index," is an index that would measure a corporation's ethical behavior. While this measurement would be hard to compile and subject to much criticism at the beginning, this much-needed measure can change the world. If we change the incentive mechanism for the business world, we will be better able to influence results in a direction toward increased social and business responsibility. With existing technology, it is now possible to create such an index. With the goodwill of leaders and people in general, it is possible to get the CEI off the ground to guide the future efforts of corporations.

Imagine reading a listing of companies ranked according to CEI, in addition to the usual ROI ranking. It would be very interesting to see the effects of this. For one thing, I would bet people would invest more heavily in companies with high CEIs and buy products and services from these companies more than those with low CEIs. The CEI could be printed on the product's packaging or service offering, so consumers consider it before making their purchasing decision. I would have no problem paying more for a product with a high CEI, and I believe a lot of people would feel the same.

Such an index is a step toward creating an incentive system

encouraging corporations to place the interests of the common citizen above the interests of shareholders. This dramatic, revolutionary change would go to the core of business, altering corporate Vision and Mission Statements, and would transform everything corporations do. Is it risky? Of course it is. Will it affect profitability? Probably in the short term, at least while the companies adapt. Profitability would definitively improve for companies with high CEIs. Consumers would be willing to pay more for products and services from these companies, and employees would have more motivation, leading to higher productivity.

As consumers, our first reaction might be: why pay more? But the reality is that today we are already paying more for everything in a system that does not work. The American consumer is paying in excess of one trillion dollars (that is a one followed by twelve zeros) toward the improprieties of the financial and business communities. We have been paying more than ever for gasoline, for health care, for air travel, and for practically every product and service we use or consume.

The CEI itself would be some type of aggregate calculation compiled by an independent organization, which would rate corporations' performance on several aspects, including: how the company treats its employees, vendors or suppliers, and its customers; how it deals with the environment; and how it behaves as a corporate citizen. The CEI would then provide some type of weighted average of these different variables.

Is it feasible? I think so. We can learn from other systems currently in use that rate services. You may be familiar with the one used by Amazon to rate books or the one used by Netflix to rate movies. In these systems, the consumer rates the book or movie on a five-point scale, and then you can see the actual accumulated results and averages. In Amazon, consumers can write their comments about a book, which is very useful for researching a book before buying.

An online system that would allow consumers to rate different corporations' products, services, and behavior would be similar. You could have different categories of ratings plus an overall rating. People could type in their comments about the corporation, and the company, in turn, could use this feedback to adjust where improvement is needed.

The feedback collected in the CEI online system would not be anonymous. My initial thinking is that people would have to identify themselves. But this requires further thought. Although employees, for example, might be hesitant to write something negative about their company, a good measure of how a company treats its employees would be the number of voluntary positive comments received.

The Corporate Ethics Foundation would be a nonprofit organization funded by individuals, corporations, or the government. Its board and management would be staffed with individuals with proven ethical track records.

So, is it possible? I hope I have convinced you that it is. If you are interested in collaborating with me on this project, please write to:

Alex Gutierrez
Corporate Ethics Foundation
P.O. Box 300
Sedona, AZ 86339-0300
www.CorporateEthicsFoundation.org

Appendix V

Marian Consecration

I, (name), a faithless sinner, renew and ratify today in your hands, O Immaculate Mother, the vows of my Baptism; I renounce forever Satan, his pomps and works; and I give myself entirely to Jesus Christ, the Incarnate Wisdom, to carry my cross after Him all the days of my life, and to be more faithful to Him than I have ever been before.

In the presence of all the heavenly court, I choose you this day for my Mother and Queen. I deliver and consecrate to you, as your slave, my body and soul, my goods, both interior and exterior, and even the value of all my good actions, past, present, and future; leaving to you the entire and full right of disposing of me, and all that belongs to me, without exception, according to your good pleasure, for the greater glory of God, in time and eternity. Amen.[1]

– St. Louis Marie de Montfort

1 Source: *True Devotion to Mary*, St. Louis Marie de Montfort. Page 198

Contact the Author:

You may contact the author by writing to:

Alex Gutierrez
P.O. Box 300,
Sedona, Arizona 86339-0300

You can also contact him through the website:
www.MotherMarysResurrection.com

or at the following e-mail:
author@MotherMarysResurrection.com

www.ingramcontent.com/pod-product-compliance
Ingram Content Group UK Ltd.
Pitfield, Milton Keynes, MK11 3LW, UK
UKHW020132250726
13967UKWH00002B/606

9 780982 324301